LEGACY LEADERSHIP

The Leader's Guide to Lasting Greatness

JEANNINE SANDSTROM • LEE SMITH

COACHWORKS PRESS

Library of Congress Control Number: 2008923867
ISBN: 978-0-9801965-0-4

First Edition

Published by:

CoachWorks® Press
Dallas, Texas
www.coachworks.com

Printed in the United States of America

To all leaders
past, present and future,
whose living legacies
inspire others to follow.

CONTENTS

Preface

Legacy Leadership® was birthed on a train speeding from one side of England to the other, written initially on the backs of napkins, ticket stubs and hotel stationery.

That was ten years ago. Since that time, we have introduced this model to the world by developing certified trainers and facilitators, and to a world of coaching clients and whole organizations who have practiced its basics and experienced its fruit. We thought it was about time to stop for a few moments, step off the speeding train and get this material to the rest of you!

In the late 1990s we authored a coach training curriculum, *The Coaching Clinic*®, which is now used globally to teach coaching skills and competencies. The train ride through England was a result of this new offering, but we knew after initial release the program would be turned over to those who train coaches, and we would be turning back to doing what we do best—executive coaching. On this long train ride our thoughts naturally inclined to this future, and subsequently to one of the greatest dilemmas we faced as executive coaches—one that persists to this day for many—and the very reason Legacy Leadership was developed.

Throughout our combined years of coaching with executives and associated leadership development, we found we did not have a complete leadership model to coach against, no comprehensive standard to measure progress or help construct a targeted yet all-inclusive development plan. Sometimes organizations had adopted certain leadership concepts which provided some techniques and tools, but often not a well-rounded scalable leadership platform. In most cases, however, these organizations didn't have a leadership model or comprehensive system. We wanted to be able to coach the whole person (and the whole organization), to help leaders deal with everything they might come up against as executives. We looked for a model that would cover all these leadership basics. We couldn't find one. Even fairly popular existing models weren't complete. Some weren't even relevant or scalable.

As the breathtaking English countryside sped by, we pondered this situation. It didn't take long for the cartoon light bulb to appear above our heads, providing light enough for us to scramble for writing materials. What were we doing sitting here lamenting something we could fix?

This was building a leadership model from the inside out, looking first at who leaders are, then what they do.

Between the two of us, our educations, experiences and years of coaching and leader development more than qualified us to construct the model we so sorely needed. And that's just what we did.

We used our experience and training in systems, behavior change, human dynamics and adult learning and leadership theory, as well as years of observing what worked and what didn't work in leadership. We began with the being of the leader, who he or she had to be, what was needed in attitude and motivation, and behaviors that would consistently and efficiently lead others to success. We were building a leadership model from the inside out, looking first at who leaders are, then what they do. We identified behavior shifts and changes, short-term and long-term motivation, internal attitudes and the human dynamics that define successful leadership—of any kind. We were building the template for a leader that lasts; not a sprinter who tires, but a marathon runner. Another light bulb revealed the concept of legacy as the pieces began coming together.

Contributing heavily to our model development were the years speeding by as quickly as the blur outside our train window. We were approaching the new millennium at this point, and we could see that everything was changing quickly, including business and leadership. Any successful leadership model must reflect these changes, especially to create legacy, and be useful and relevant in an ever transitioning and morphing business environment.

> Great leaders intentionally influence and develop other leaders... In other words, they become Legacy Leaders building a multi-generational thumbprint for others who will use these same principles...

The old "command and control" style of leadership won't work anymore. Smart workers expect more and different competencies from their leaders, and more reason for them to excel than merely producing profit for someone else. Employees expect leaders to be interested in them, and not just the bottom line. Long-term corporate loyalty was becoming a thing of the past, with workers holding more positions and making more career changes than ever before. They also generally handle more responsibilities.

Today's global competition demands top talent, and leadership needs to attract and retain the best in the workforce. Perhaps one of the biggest changes, and one that is most difficult to address, is the fact that technology is unfolding so quickly that the maturing process for leadership development has been short-circuited. Today's workers, and especially young executives, have not had the opportunity to grow the vital people skills required for leadership. They have not been allowed to become seasoned. We knew that great leaders intentionally influence and develop other leaders, build teams and foster collaborative cultures. In other words, they become Legacy Leaders, building a multi-generational thumbprint for others who will use these same principles of learning and training with their own staff members.

As the model came together, what emerged was a system that fits the need for great leadership in good times or bad times, in fast times or slow times. These leaders don't have to be super human, but they do need a sincere desire, and knowledge, to be a great leader. They need a leadership framework. This framework, or leadership platform, is what we term Legacy Leadership, the Five Legacy Practices, with guidelines to shape competencies and behaviors and attitudes. Legacy Leader skills are designed to be flexible in any situation, and are focused on interactions with other people to accomplish goals.

Business is always future-paced. Leadership shifts need to be purposeful, and that purpose is to impact the future, to influence others, to shift from just-in-time (or just-in-case) learning to real-time application for current and future success. As we coach executives, the most sustainable work has been through identifying gaps that needed filling, and then working with the client to create strategies, and to develop attitudes, behaviors and motivations that can fill and bridge these gaps. The foundational context for this process has become Legacy Leadership. Our executive coaching is not about fixing the past, but about creating a new future. Our work with individual leaders and entire organizations is focused on the future, whether five minutes or five years from now. It is about building bridges to tomorrow. The Five Legacy Practices enable this kind of successful coaching strategy. This model is not linear, and does not depend on starting at the beginning. It can be implemented at any place in the leader's development, and at any place in the model. It is highly flexible and adaptable to just about any leadership need, anyplace, anytime. And by its very nature, it builds the leaders of tomorrow.

Legacy Leadership is a brand. It defines leaders, who they are, and what they do.

Companies are concerned about branding today. Branding is a unique distinction that sets you apart from any other person, or any other company. It speaks to who you are, what you do, what your product is. It is generally recognizable in a few words. Legacy Leadership is a brand. It defines the leader, who he or she is, and what they do. Once leaders embrace the concepts and platform of Legacy Leadership, everything they do comes out of the Five Legacy Practices. They are intentional, moving from unconscious competence to conscious greatness. We cannot not influence. We can't prevent people from talking about us. The challenge as leaders is to be intentional, creating and living that talk now—living our *legacy* now, in real time. It is intentional influence that shapes the future. This is our leadership legacy—our brand.

A lot of Legacy Leaders have been developed over the past ten years, and we have enjoyed seeing the results of their transitions. That is the reason this book hasn't been completed earlier. We have been too busy working with executive leaders, establishing a proven profile of performance for Legacy Leadership. We have taken this model into large and small organizations, with emerging and existing leaders, both resistant and open to learning new leadership competencies. In every case, the model has stood the test of time and the test of changing leadership trends and business conditions. Individual leaders have been transformed into dynamic Legacy Leaders, living their leadership legacy daily, and continuing to demonstrate unlimited growth and unprecedented results. Organizations have been shifted to entire Legacy Leadership cultures where all Five Legacy Practices are evident, contributing to impressive returns on the investment of leadership development. In some cases growth was swift and impressive. In others, it has been a slow but steady course toward living legacy. Each leader and each organization is different and unique, and each will respond in varying ways. Much depends on the mind set of the individuals, and the desire to be and do their personal, professional and organizational best. We have included case studies from our years of coaching to Legacy Leadership in this book. Each chapter contains examples of our application of the model with real leaders.

We have been asked often why this model works so well. The answer is simple, just like the model. It is a blend of the technology of human interaction (business is about relationships) and sound business practices. It defines what works in human dynamics, and details what is necessary for business success. Ten years after its birth it has left its own legacy—a consistent track record and experiential evidence that it works.

Having a solid comprehensive leadership development tool, and a platform on which to base leadership excellence, may have been the motivating factors in the design of this model. When we coach executives, however, our purpose is not just to develop a better leader who can better him- or herself, but to grow a leader of legacy who can impact all those who follow, whether in business or in life. Legacy Leaders make the world around them a better place. Like the ripples on a lake, everyone is touched as the influence spreads. Our purpose is to enable leaders to find and develop *their* leadership purpose, and live it fully, everywhere.

What will be your business or leadership legacy? How do you want people to remember you and your leadership years from now? What will your reputation be? Isn't it about time to start living that legacy today, intentionally shaping your legacy for tomorrow? Welcome to Legacy Leadership. This is our legacy to you.

Lee and Jeannine
January 2008

Something to consider as you read this book...

"Our achievements of today are but
the sum total of our thoughts of yesterday.
You are today where the thoughts of yesterday
have brought you and you will be tomorrow
where the thoughts of today take you."

—*Blaise Pascal*
French Philosopher, Mathematician and Physicist (mid-1600s)

LEGACY LEADERSHIP

**The Leader's Guide to
Lasting Greatness**

Introduction to Legacy Leadership

What is Legacy?

How do you define *legacy*? It's a word we hear bouncing and buzzing frequently around bookstores and TV talk shows these days. It was originally thought to imply the fortune, or lack thereof, that one would *leave behind* for his or her heirs. Today it has come to signify what people are known for, how they are remembered after their passing. Do you know what your legacy will be? Will it be something you are remembered for only when you're gone? What if you were *living* your legacy now? What if your vision for the future, your legacy, is evident in everything you do, every day? It can happen. Legacy Leadership is about *living* your legacy, not just *leaving* it.

> It's who we are and what we live today that shapes our legacy for tomorrow.

Living your legacy means making a dedicated investment in the better future of others. This isn't about money, financial investment or material wealth and capital building. Legacy Leadership is not about building things. It is about building people. It is about investing your time, your energy, your competencies and your interest and concern in individuals who then share what they have learned with others, maximizing the return on your investment. While this book is primarily concerned with leadership legacy in business, this simple formula for human investment is applicable to every area of life—family, community, *and* business. Each of us can be a leader in our respective environments. In a basic sense, a leader is one who shows the way, who escorts or guides others. A *Legacy* Leader guides others into a better future—into *being* better, *doing* better, and *leading* better. Your best self is offered to others in order to develop their best selves and so on, leaving a multi-generational imprint—a living legacy.

Legacy Leaders

We can all tell stories or remember details about the lives, careers, and accomplishments of noted leaders today and in history. While there were,

> It seems that Legacy Leaders all have the SAME right stuff.

and are, many good or excellent leaders among us, only certain greats garner a sort of language and emotion that separates them from other leaders, creating lasting influence. If you listen carefully, you will hear it too. The stories are laced with the *language of legacy*—captured in the 5 Practices of Legacy Leadership. We call these men and women Legacy Leaders. And it seems that Legacy Leaders all have the *same* right stuff.

Some of these leaders are known well, and draped in titles, medals, decorations, awards, achievements and accomplishments. These are impressive and noteworthy, but do not make the Legacy Leader. Some are high profile; others remain behind the scenes. Some are businesspeople; others are not. We can tell you stories of dozens of men and women, everyday folks, who have profoundly influenced others and lived lives of true leadership legacy. They don't all share the public eye, and they don't all have an arm's-length list of noted accomplishments. What they *do* all have is the same stuff that makes a leader a *Legacy* Leader. This is what Legacy Leadership is all about—identifying and defining the right stuff of leaders of legacy.

Legacy Leaders are found in every walk of life, from the boardroom to the battlefield, from public service to private homes, neighborhoods, schools and communities. They are found in the worn pages of history books, the memories of those who have been touched by them, and they continue to inspire and influence present and future leaders.

Recognized or relatively unknown, in business or life in general, the world is hungry for these kind of leaders—*Legacy* Leaders. They are leaders who intentionally influence others. Influencing is at the core of their being, and drives the behaviors, skills and competencies of all the practices of Legacy Leadership. It is what allows the leader to live his or her legacy today, and to grow the leaders of tomorrow. In small ways, or grand strokes, these leaders change our world.

Legacy and Influence

> We cannot NOT influence.

Legacy in leadership is not about leaving something behind—it is about influencing others enough to cause change, a shift from unconsciously doing leadership to consciously *being* a leader. The best way to do that is to influence in person, by living legacy today, not waiting for others to reflect on the past tomorrow.

We all influence, whether we know it or not. In fact, we cannot *not* influence. *Whether* we influence is not the question. It's *how* we influence—

positively or negatively, intentionally or accidentally. Are we mindful and conscious about influence, or completely unaware of our impact on others? Many think of influencing only as a method to obtain what they want. This is not the kind of influence we're discussing here. They are merely *using* influence to gain power, money, favor, status or whatever it is that satisfies *self*. This is an important distinction. Using influence for self-centered gain is deception. Intentionally influencing for selfless positive relationships and growth is legacy.

Influence is the heart of legacy. Understanding how your personal and professional legacy of influence works is critical to understanding Legacy Leadership, and critical to positively impacting others. A strong, positive person of intentional influence possesses a demeanor, a certain knowing, and an instant and irresistible attraction or connection with others. We are reminded of a tribute we read of the passing of such a leader: *"... someone who quickly and easily earned my respect ... there was an intangible about him in this way unlike anyone I have ever met."* Intentional influence is a characteristic and attitude that draws people. This individual called the leader's influence an "intangible." We would give this intangible a name— *presence*.

There's a lot to be said for the power of presence. You have most likely known people like this—those with whom you desired company, learning and acceptance. And the most peculiar thing about these people is that others seem to want to work hard to please them, to be their best selves, be more like them. There is a saying that captures this quality: *"Our best friends are those in whose presence we can be our best selves."* People who positively influence are those in whose presence we can be our best selves, do our best work, and reach our best potential.

What are the characteristics of a person who influences, one with this kind of *presence*? Consider the people who have influenced you most in life. What characteristics did these people have? Chances are your list will include most of what Legacy Leadership comprises.

We are obliged to offer one note of caution. A person who positively and intentionally influences others is not just someone who makes everyone *feel good*. They will often have to deliver tough talk, or ask tough questions, or make tough decisions that impact others. However, this toughness will be delivered with such humility and committed resolve for the best outcomes for everyone, that people will naturally and consistently be inspired and led by them—to be their best selves. Their presence in the lives of people leaves lasting impact.

What is Legacy Leadership?

Over the many years of our combined experience, we have observed the most common behaviors of successful leaders and identified the Legacy Practices that set outstanding leaders apart from other leaders. When we listened to the deepest issues that were on leaders' minds, they were matters of meaning and legacy. We developed Legacy Leadership as a map for ensuring excellence in leadership practices that would enable leaders to not only leave the legacy they intended—but to *live* it today.

We have isolated, defined and made transferable the practices common to leaders who are able to achieve and sustain success—with people, product and revenue. Legacy Leadership is based on five Legacy Practices which are common in all great leaders, whether it be the ancients whose successes leap from the worn pages of history, or the Fortune 500 leaders of today—and will be observed in the leaders of tomorrow. It is a philosophy, a model, and a proven process for bringing out individual best, developing leaders in an organization, establishing organizational leadership culture, and positively impacting the bottom line. It is a balanced approach to people and production. It is simple, yet powerful—it works.

Current leader books and articles cover various aspects and techniques of leadership, yet do not deliver a comprehensive model. Legacy Leadership is a complete framework of practices, behaviors, attitudes and values that addresses every aspect of successful leadership, energizes people and whole organizations, and actively grows tomorrow's leaders, today. *Legacy* Leaders become students of leadership while focusing on building other leaders who build leaders, who build leaders....

We hear stories every day about the lack of strong leadership talent. Legacy Leadership is a broad platform for developing such talented leaders. It includes competencies and practices with immediate applicability to most every possibility and challenge leaders face today.

Many organizations have a set of competencies with which to measure their leader performance; others do not. In either case, Legacy Leadership provides a sound structure in which such competencies can reside. The five Legacy Practices form a structural map for a full and complete picture of your leader development program's destination, for you personally and for those you lead. The outcome is fully developed leaders, both current and emerging, and a greatly enhanced leadership potential within the organization. Legacy Leadership makes it easy to embrace a powerful leadership system throughout an organization by providing the guidelines and simple framework for individuals to sustain that culture. It was originally designed for leadership development—at all levels. Every employee is a potential leader, capable of becoming a true Legacy Leader. This system outlines and defines the way the organization does business—in every meeting, every operation, every project, every person at every level.

Legacy Leadership is not a leadership style—it is a life system and a way of *being,* not just *doing.* This system contains the wisdom of the ages structured and packaged for today's—and tomorrow's—leaders. Its truths and practices are timeless, proven keys to sustained significance—and form the foundation for real-time legacy in today's business environment. The model is vital and highly adaptable. Legacy Leadership contains reliable, time-honored principles refined into an intentional, powerful system for success—today and tomorrow—for self and for others.

The Five Legacy Practices

Given that leadership can be complex, we have simplified and distinguished five core competency platforms which represent a complete set of observable and measurable behaviors. The behaviors, when used in total, are leverage points for success. We included those practices of leadership that are essential for every leader, regardless of industry or position within the organization. We call these the 5 Legacy Practices. Most major leadership models or approaches will find a fit within this balanced and comprehensive framework. A simple model illustrates this framework.

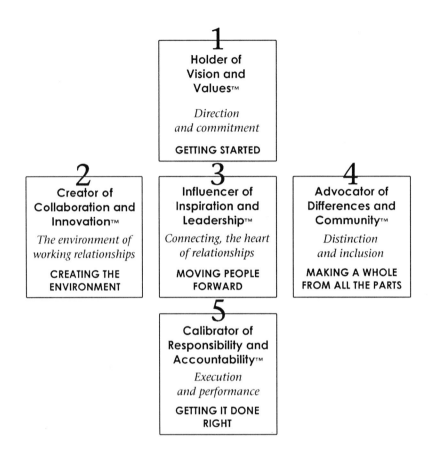

Being and Doing

Each of the 5 Legacy Practices has three components: one part *being*, and two parts *doing*. Most leadership models have a list of competencies, skills and actions that contribute to good leadership. *Great* leaders, however, don't just *do*, they *are*. Too often people focus merely on the *doing* of leadership. It is vital to consider both aspects of *being* and *doing*. *Being* a leader involves a certain consciousness, awareness of who the leader is, and how this awareness and core of being drive leadership actions and behavior. As we initially sought to title the 5 Legacy Practices, it became increasingly difficult to apply a simple label to include all the inherent components. We finally settled on titles that actually said what was meant, and were not merely coined terms or jargon.

When we applied our labels to these Legacy Practices, we took some initial flack about the names. We were told they weren't "trendy" enough, or that they were too wordy. We honestly tried to determine other titles that would be as memorable as these, but we found that nothing else perfectly defines these practices as well as the simple words that define their *being* and *doing*. After ten years of these labels, we're glad we stuck with them. Leaders remember them, and use them to guide their actions. A trendy piece of jargon won't do that. Here's what we call the 5 Legacy Practices of Legacy Leadership:

One:	Holder of Vision and Values™
Two:	Creator of Collaboration and Innovation™
Three:	Influencer of Inspiration and Leadership™
Four:	Advocator of Differences and Community™
Five:	Calibrator of Responsibility and Accountability™

The first word in each title is the *being* part of that leadership practice. A great leader is first a holder, a creator, an influencer, an advocator and a calibrator. This is the key to understanding this leadership model, and to understanding what really makes leaders great. The greatness resides in *who they are* first, and *what they do* second. What a person does is dictated by who they are. Some people will debate about whether a leader is born or created. We say it is a little of both. It begins with the core of the leader— who he or she is. But even this core nature can be shaped and transformed.

[handwritten margin note: 1st who they are - and do]

Sometimes it is about having what we often call an "attitude adjustment." We've all had those, and often these adjustments can alter who we are in the future. This is the purpose of this model, to shape the leader's core being, and then polish how he or she acts out that being.

What is in This Book

This book is essentially presented in two parts. The first part is a discussion of the 5 Legacy Practices. Part two is your opportunity to take what you learn and put it to work.

PART ONE: The Legacy Practices

Each of the Legacy Practices is detailed in the following five chapters. The chapter titles reflect the positive action of the *being* part of the practice:

Chapter 1: Holding Vision and Values
(Setting the Stage)

Chapter 2: Creating Collaboration and Innovation
(Creating the Environment)

Chapter 3: Influencing Inspiration and Leadership
(Moving People Forward)

Chapter 4: Advocating Differences and Community
(Making a Whole From All the Parts)

Chapter 5: Calibrating Responsibility and Accountability
(Getting It Done Right)

PART TWO: Next Steps: DEVELOPMENT GUIDE

To make the most of the legacy chapters, and to enhance your learning, a "Development Guide" is found in the Appendix of this book. The Guide is also separated into the 5 Legacy Practices and contains opportunities for you to take your leadership to a more intentional, influential and legacy-building level. This guide is like a *companion workbook*. It is completely up to you what, if any, part of it you use for your personal and professional leadership growth. The contents and suggested use of this companion piece are found in the introductory pages of the Development Guide.

At the end of each legacy chapter you will find a reminder note about the Guide and a quick listing of what you will find there. We've also included a few "starter" questions at the end of each chapter. We hope Part Two of this book will be a valuable addition to your leadership learning.

Chapter

ONE

Legacy Practice 1

1
Holder of Vision and Values™

2
Creator of Collaboration and Innovation™

3
Influencer of Inspiration and Leadership™

4
Advocator of Differences and Community™

5
Calibrator of Responsibility and Accountability™

With the torch of vision held firmly in one hand, the path ahead is clearly seen. With the beacon of values grasped in the other, we successfully negotiate the curving passes and expansive valleys to arrive safely at our destination. Lay either light down, even for a moment, and all can be lost over the unseen cliffs ahead.

ONE: Legacy Practice 1

SETTING THE STAGE
Holding Vision
and Values

1

Construction sites around the world,
whether multi-million dollar towers
to the sun or mere modest abodes,
have one thing in common.

You will find this universal commonality in various places and in various
conditions. They can be seen rolled and tucked under the arms of foremen,
inspectors, plumbers and architects. They are found crudely nailed to
exposed wall studs. They are professionally generated, or doodled on a pad
of paper. They are scribbled on, spattered on, torn and dog-eared. But they
are always there. We are speaking of course of the blueprints, or plans for
whatever structure is under construction. They began as a vision or dream,
were given life on paper, and then used to create everything from the amaz-
ingly grand to the oh-so-humble edifice.

One thing is always certain—everyone, from the dreamers,
financiers, architects, supervisors, inspectors and construction managers—on

down to the individual tradesperson or laborer—either carries these plans or has them readily accessible. This "paper vision" is constantly present, continuously referenced, and consistently used to guide construction. Without these plans the structure cannot be built. Any deviation from these plans is only through formal channels and authorizations. Performance and outcomes are always measured by these plans. Regardless of project size or expense, building plans are the one single common ground for all structures. But as grand the role these plans play, they are merely pieces of paper, and are without any power unless "held" by the people making them come alive.

The architect of the project holds the plans close to be certain the structure rises as visioned. The inspector holds and references the plans to guarantee the work is done correctly and within all stated specifications and codes. The individual workers hold the plans to be sure that every last nail, board, steel beam, rivet, bolt and screw is installed in the right place, at the right time, in the right way. And the project investors hold the plans to ensure what they have financed is indeed what has been built. In other words, they glue everything together—including people and processes—but only when embraced, encouraged and enforced.

The Holder of Vision and Values is *each one* of these people, using the plans—the vision and values—to guide and direct all activities in the building of the organization. Like the architect, the foreman, the banker and the laborer, the leader holds the vision secure, and operates within the specified values. Organizational position matters little here, as all employees need to embrace and hold the vision and values of any company to ensure its success, just as every worker on any structure does with building plans. And as with all leadership competencies and behaviors, it begins—and ends—with the leader.

Values

Do you have a vision? Have you stated company values and guiding principles? Good, but not good enough. Simply writing down vision and subsequent goals, and suggesting values, only to have them remain tucked away in the dark and musty annals of corporate policy manuals does not serve their intended purpose. Even mounting them on the walls for all to see makes no difference. They are to be integrated into all behavior, strategies, relationships and daily operations, so they will guide and direct the processes to achieve results. In other words, they are intentionally *held—kept in hand, embraced and encouraged.* Great leaders, Legacy Leaders, are conscious guardians of both personal and organizational vision and values. It becomes part of who they are, and guides all they do. They understand the necessity of never allowing vision and values to slip out of focus or priority. A great leader, a leader whose leadership lasts and stands the test of time, is very clear about his or her own core vision and values— personally, professionally and organizationally—and lives them, preserves them and relies upon them as a guide. Doing so sets the stage for all other components of leadership. Without this aspect of leadership, the other parts cannot survive.

> **Great leaders are conscious guardians of both personal and organizational vision and values. This guardianship becomes part of who they are, and guides all they do.**

Herb Kelleher, co-founder, Chairman and former CEO of Southwest Airlines, has been quoted and referenced often in the past years as a bright shining star of leadership, and has been called perhaps the best CEO in America by *Fortune* magazine. There's very good reason for that. In the early days of Southwest Airlines, employees said you could find Mr. Kelleher everywhere in the company, spreading the vision, reinforcing the values

quote

and holding the ideas for all to see of what was envisioned for the company. No one had any confusion about where the company was going. Everyone saw the light cast on the successful path of Southwest Airlines. Everyone in the organization, regardless of position, could tell you exactly what the company's vision was, and the values it represented, in everything it did. Employees worked with a consistent set of vision and values, lived by its leader, modeled as an example of what to work toward, and how to work. The results of this holding of vision and values speak loudly to this day in the unprecedented success of this airline, especially when others were struggling just to survive.

If you are thinking that you have to be the CEO to hold vision and values, think again. *Every leader* is responsible for knowing and holding these components vital to organizational success, and implementing and executing them within their areas of responsibility. At every level within the company, each leader acting as the holder of vision and values is a light that shines consistently, helping others see the path and get to where they have determined to go—successfully and safely. The light does not shine in areas where the path should not be followed, but it does illuminate consistent vision and values as path markers, showing direction. We could spend pages describing vision, but quite simply, vision is a clear view and understanding of realizable goals, plans and intentions. Every organization, at every level, has some sort of vision or plan for their existence. It is what defines success for that organization, or even for each individual. The most difficult part of vision is distilling down the various details into a well-crafted and understood light on the path to success. Vision is where the leader operates. Great leaders *live today* the legacy they want to leave tomorrow.

> **Vision is a clear view and an understanding of realizable goals, plans and intentions.**

A Holder of Vision has clear knowledge and alignment with the organization's vision, and its relationship with all individuals, teams and activities. This leader brings his or her whole self to this leadership model, provides consistent focus and direction and helps the vision come alive in everyday activities. *Legacy* Leaders consistently communicate, strategize around, and measure performance against, the established organizational vision. This vision is the foundational purpose for all efforts. Leaders of legacy actually make the vision exciting.

Values are those things considered right, worthwhile, and desirable—the basis of guiding principles and standards. The importance of values cannot be overstated. Values and beliefs drive culture, and all of human behavior, becoming guiding principles around which we work with employees, customers, vendors and the community.

The Legacy Leader holds values by understanding and encouraging the consistent use of organizational guiding principles that are observable, measurable and replicable by others. Holders of Values protect personal and organizational values from becoming eroded or ignored. They model authenticity—their personal and professional lives are seamless. Personal values and organizational values need to match, or the employee and the employer do not match. Legacy Leaders encourage others to develop, define and live personal and organizational values, and enjoy values-driven achievement.

In order to successfully *hold vision* there is first a clear and compelling organizational vision, in writing, communicated throughout the company. There is a road map to success (strategic plan), ways to measure the vision (established milestones) and consistent accountability. *Holding values* begins with a set of fully developed and clearly defined values or guiding principles, communicated and reinforced throughout the organization. Just like vision, values require measurement methods, employee clarity and acceptance, and an attitude of working according to values promoted which underlie all work.

Make it Meaningful

You might be surprised how many organizations do not have a stated or written vision. Even if such a vision exists, the critical next step of ensuring understanding, commitment and ownership of the vision by all team members is often ignored. Visions may also need to be periodically evaluated and re-crafted. It might be time to gather the executive team together and develop a vision that will drive your organization, and to be sure every member of the organization knows it. But this Legacy Practice is not just about *having* a vision, it's about *reinforcing* it on a daily basis in everything you do, and then holding yourself accountable for this behavior.

In order to obtain employee buy-in of vision and values, however, they need to be more than lofty (or dusty!) ideals full of nice-sounding words or technical jargon. People are driven by emotional responses to what is considered important and of value—and what they personally relate to. An organization that has achieved any level of success at meeting its vision and operating with values has most likely also collected some stories along the way that relate to this success. For example, a medical device company may have pioneered an innovative piece of equipment that was actually credited with saving lives—real people. Or an investment company may have spearheaded a huge gain that enabled some amazing client achievement. Every company has its success stories. Develop and use these to help relate corporate vision to real people. These are real stories that can drive home and reinforce vision and values, and make them more *accessible* and *"ownable"* than a merely official printed mission statement. Use your success stories to reinforce your organization's vision and values, and craft them to relate to every employee, not just senior-level executives. Give them "redeemable" merit—in other words, make your vision, and the values by which the organization works, worthwhile and meaningful. Help ensure that people will *want* to work to this vision, and with these values.

Many people think designing a vision is easy—just selecting a few nice and impressive words to share with your adoring public. In other words, they think visioning is soft. Wrong. The blueprints and plans for any building are highly detailed,

> Having a strong vision means knowing who you are.

professional and specific about what that building will look like, and what will make it strong enough to last. Having a strong vision means knowing who you are, and exactly what you want to do, then consistently setting out to achieve it, according to your plan, being vigilant to hold everyone accountable and nimble enough to make changes or course corrections. Abandoning any part of this process will lead to unfilled vision, and meaningless values.

Integrating Vision

After the vision is drafted and communicated, there is a critical action required before any fulfillment can be realized—*integration*. Integration means bringing all the individual pieces of vision, all the departments, steps, processes, phases, teams and individuals together and incorporating them into a unified and harmonious whole.

Every part of building construction—foundation, framing, plumbing, flooring, roofing, electrical and so on—has a set of plans to complete individual functions within guidelines, that team's part of the envisioned building. Likewise, every area of the organization is not only fully aware of the vision, but also consciously and intentionally integrates it into daily function. Integrating vision means putting it to work as a driving force, the foundation for decision making, the guiding light for all activities. Vision is not found in a book on a shelf, or framed on a wall. It is seen every day in every department, in every worker, in every activity. It is that light on the path. It is difficult to travel, or work, in the dark. The light of organizational vision is on all the time, bright and clear. It is repeated, reinforced, revisited and blended with daily routine.

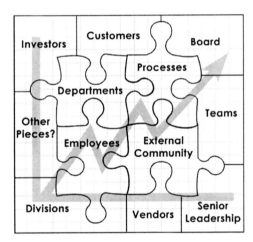

INTEGRATED VISION AND VALUES

Think about the word "integration." Integration implies an incorporated harmony of all parts. Consider how your work, your language, and your attitude can show that organizational vision has been integrated, obvious by your actions and behavior. It is also important to determine if your *personal* goals and vision are integrated with that of your organization. If they are not, it is quite possible that you and your organization are working at odds to one another, and that you personally have not made a commitment to the organization's vision. If you are working under these conditions, you may need to ask yourself tough questions and provide some even tougher answers.

Strategic Plans:
The Legs of Vision

In order to reinforce, integrate and model vision or values effectively, it is vital to have a strategic plan. Vision is like the architectural rendering of how a building will look when completed. Strategic plans are the steps involved in constructing every part of that building—or business. Without such a plan, a vision is merely a dream without legs. Vision is where you want to go. The strategic plan is how to get from where you are, to where you want to be. Vision is translated into end goals, measurable and achievable with a plan of action. The strategic plan is coupled with direct accomplishment of vision. One cannot work without the other. You may have the horse, and the buggy, but neither will carry you, and those with you, to your destination alone. The Legacy Leader will combine a well-defined vision with strategic thinking and a plan to get from here to there.

> The entrepreneurial founder of a small investment group led his company very successfully for 30 years using his directive style of leadership.

He made the decisions and told his people what to do. He was able to attract very good people around him, and through his directive style, trained them to be able to change and adapt with his direction. When the company reached a higher level of success, with larger, more complex projects and more decisions than he could personally make on his own, he had to retrain the top leaders to think for themselves. He began leading the company with a more collaborative than directive style of leadership. To get all the troops on-board and moving in the same direction, strategic planning was critical—the bottom line was now in the hundreds of millions of dollars. Leaders needed to follow a plan, not wait for directions as they had before. The goals were bigger, the deals more complex, the stakes were larger, and dispersed action no longer worked. He found that associated action plans within a strategic plan were the key ingredients. As the company integrated a more thoughtful strategy into the more complex organization, people began measuring every action they took against the stated vision. They were able to reach the goals more quickly as a team, because everyone was on board with the strategic plan and actively working toward it—instead of awaiting orders from the general.

It is clear that vision is to be teamed with strategy. And operational strategy for every functional area has a line of sight directly to the organization's vision. Every leader is responsible for devising a plan to achieve the organization's vision within his or her area of responsibility. That plan, however, does not stop with you. Strategic plans are "broadcast" to your entire team. If you are the CEO, that broadcast is organization-wide. If not, your team or area of responsibility is your broadcast range. Clear communication is essential, but this is only the beginning. You enable your team to translate the organization's vision for applicability in your area of responsibility, on a daily basis.

Marge was a mover and shaker in the consultancy where she worked.

Her weakness, however, was her lack of understanding of the critical and complex nature of her group's follow-through on sales. She often procrastinated on follow-through and modeled that behavior for her team. Realizing that there may be a gap between daily responsibilities and holding the vision of the company, Marge gathered the team together to establish how the group could relate more readily to the vision by determining how each person's role contributed to getting things done. Through a suggestion from a team member, they agreed that every morning each person would write down the top three things that needed to be done that day, and how each daily goal aligned with the organizational goals. Marge and the team tried this for the first month and re-evaluated their progress. They found that when they all understood how each person uniquely contributed to the results of the team's accomplishments, and how they depended on each other for success, the level of procrastination decreased, and production increased. Now daily responsibilities aligned fully with organizational vision and goals.

Benjamin Disraeli said, *"The secret of success is constancy of purpose."* This is very appropriate to the subject of vision and values, especially translating and aligning the organization's vision with daily area responsibilities. Give thought to what will be your "constancy of purpose" and how you will align it with the company's strategic plan—consistently.

Measurement

You know the vision. You have a strategic plan. You have communicated clearly and helped your team translate the vision and align it with daily responsibilities. Now what? How will you know if you are successfully accomplishing the vision? The next step is setting the standards and identifying the measurable milestones and benchmarks that will serve as your guide on the path to successfully accomplishing your organizational vision.

Doug is the division manager of a major energy company.

He had always been of the mind that all his people needed to know was the vision, and he pretty much left them to figure out how to get things done. Doug's style of hands-off management was not working, and his division was often at the bottom of production in meeting overall company goals. During a performance appraisal, he received strong feedback about this, as well as a directive to turn his group around. Doug was a valuable asset to his organization, and they engaged an executive coach to facilitate this turnaround. Working with his coach, Doug determined that even though it wasn't his style, he needed to hold himself and others accountable by adding shorter-term goals, or milestones, to keep his division on track. The team worked together to establish strong monthly and quarterly measurements to determine how much progress (or lack thereof) had been made. In this way, he could report to corporate regularly how close they were to growing their area of the business. Over one year's time, Doug implemented this milestone approach and his group's production moved beyond their originally stated goals. He not only saved his job, but contributed greatly to his company's profit for the year, and redesigned how his division worked toward goals.

Values

Without the measurement markers, you and your team have no way of knowing concretely if your work has accomplished, or is accomplishing, the vision. Without measuring the structure against the original blueprints, you have no way of knowing if you have built what was planned and envisioned. You can't manage what you can't—or don't—measure. It's that simple. Try listing at least five different key performance indicators, along with timelines or due dates that you and your team will use to confirm that you are—or take actions when you are not—accomplishing the vision and strategy in your respective areas of responsibility. Your performance indicators determine how you will measure your success against these markers, and how you will correct any "misalignments." Get specific. Develop policies and procedures that can be followed consistently. Although responsibility and accountability are competencies associated with Legacy Practice Five for this model, they are critical to meeting vision and are necessarily detailed in your process plan.

Living the Values

The term *values* implies a set of guiding principles that serve as a navigational and behavioral beacon for your organization. Guiding principles are intended to shape the organization's culture. If these values are not currently present, consider a collaborative effort to draft such a set of guiding principles. Collaboration in establishing values brings ownership and buy-in, rather than a skeptical attitude about someone else's "rules." If you do have established values (a written set of guiding principles), consider how you can *reinforce* the values of this organization, and your personal

> Values are a navigational and behavioral beacon.

values, in a practical day-to-day manner within your functional area. Values are to be modeled, displayed, serve as an example, and show what is typical and desired. And this behavior is intentional. Leaders who live their legacy will model values with purpose, firmly and with steadfastness, and sharply focused design. In other words, with intention.

Many large and small companies publicly promote their vision and values. Many are proud of their clever or impressive language. Here's one notable, succinct and highly publicized set of values: "*Communication, Respect, Integrity, Excellence.*" Sounds good, doesn't it? Unfortunately these impressive values were never integrated and certainly were not intentionally modeled in this organization. The company? Enron, whose leaders made the organization's values a world-wide brunt of jokes that spelled disaster. The ripple effect of this lack of living and modeling values had far-reaching implications which have affected all other organizations in some way. It takes far more than merely having a list of values. It takes intentional focus and integration into all organizational activities—by everyone.

Responsibility and accountability standards for abiding by organizational values need to have previous thought and known policies that clearly state what will happen if company values are not observed. You need to know ahead of time how you will handle breaches. If not, each infraction ignored is like a little more erosion in the levee holding back the waters of destruction and failure. Without diligent attention, ignored values and guidelines will eventually, at some point usually unknown, lead to complete dam failure, allowing the flood waters to surge in and wipe out what once may have been a strong and values-driven organization.

Core Values

Your behavior is driven by your personal values set, whether you are aware of it or not. This set of values comprises what you consider true, valid and important about your personal and professional life. It is much easier to do the "right thing" or uphold values when you know in advance what you stand for. Most people assume they already have a set of clearly defined values, but may not have taken the time to delineate and clarify them in order to know how they will respond in certain situations. As a practical exercise, try listing at least five core values in your *personal* life and in your *professional* life. Try to make these five core values express who you are, and what is important to you. It's not as easy as it sounds, but the exercise alone can be life changing and core strengthening. Read over your ten statements (five for each of the two areas above) several times. Now consider what you need to do in order to consistently "walk the talk" of your stated values, and how you will handle potential conflicts in either of these areas. Consider how you can prepare to handle challenges or changes in your personal life, and in your professional and organizational life. Handling change with grace and ease requires a changeless core inside you. Solidify your values, integrate them into daily activities, and establish them as boundaries and markers to guide future behavior.

Intentionally Living Your Values Enables You To:

- Solidify your guiding principles to guide daily behavior

- Be congruent and consistent

- Be intentional about your leadership

- Determine alignment (or lack of alignment) with organizational values

- Behave honestly

- Be your real self

- Have a solid foundation for all decisions and actions

It is important for you, and your team members, to have clearly identified personal values, and to always work in alignment with those values, especially as they relate to your work in your organization. Identifying your values, and intentionally walking them daily are keys to real success.

If you are to be a leader of integrity, a *Legacy* Leader, your personal and professional lives are to be seamless. Your behaviors and attitudes do not change when you put on the business suit, or "change back" when you leave the building. A Legacy Leader does not assume a persona like a super-hero dons a cape. He or she is that leader, and lives those values, no matter where, when or what. The leader's "walk" is grounded in and aligned with the leader's "talk" and does not alter itself to adapt to the environment like a chameleon. A leader of integrity is a person of integrity, and looks the same in every place, at every time. And besides all that, it's too stressful to live an incongruent life. That's one area of stress that you can indeed control and even eliminate. Just be who you are—everywhere.

Integrating Values

Intentionally modeling values is the beginning of integration, but not the end. A leader can model values and guiding principles, yet just as for vision, the values need to be integrated into organizational culture before they can ground how the company works. Every area of the organization embraces and integrates the stated values into how they do business—and *ensures* that this integration happens.

Dan was a highly creative leader, with a track record of success.

He was recently hired by a large development corporation to lead a team to create new investments and joint ventures. This organization had a strong value of "doing the right thing" which meant that new investments were measured by the corporate values of integrity and honesty present in all deals. Unfortunately, Dan's personal values did not match those of the corporation. Dan placed a higher value on making the deal, no matter what. The first major transaction he brought to the table for decision was the purchase of an older building. In order to make the deal, Dan led the seller to believe that the building would be preserved and renovated, which was very important to the seller. Dan's real intent, however, was to remove the building and erect a highrise. When Dan's executive board met to discuss the potential purchase, they discovered his lack of integrity. His "bait and switch" approach did not match the company's values for integrity in the deal. The corporate brand would be greatly tarnished in the process. It was more important that the company's value of "doing the right thing" be preserved than either the deal or Dan's job. The deal was denied and so was Dan.

> Speak what you value, and do it repeatedly.

It is important to plan ahead for the actions you will take in the event that the organization's values are not integrated and applied successfully to all business practices. Address these issues with all team members, and set accountabilities in place. This development company's brand and values were more important than making a deal. It is vital for you and your organization to know where you stand, and what you will do, in a similar situation.

We've heard "practice what you preach" since childhood. Today's version is "walk your talk." For the integration of values, however, it is just as important to *preach* what you practice, or *talk* what you walk. In other words, speak what you value, and do it *repeatedly*. If the organization in the example above had communicated clearly (and yes, even *preached*) its values and guiding principles on a more consistent basis, including the importance of integrity in the overall driving values of the company, perhaps Dan would not have chosen to compromise them, and maybe he would not have even been hired in the first place. Integrating values means spreading them at all levels—employees, vendors and suppliers, customers, shareholders and the public. Spreading includes preaching and practicing.

Developing Potential:
The Key to True Legacy

What does the development of others have to do with holding vision and values? Everything! Developing others, working at discovering the potential leadership qualities of your team members, is essential to

> A Legacy Leader is always thinking in tomorrows, while firmly standing in today.

the organizational vision and success. Not everyone may possess the skills, abilities and potential to be a great leader, but everyone will benefit from someone intentionally working to develop that person's potential— and ultimately the organization's vision is advanced. An organization's vision depends on the constant growth of its workers. The business world is a rapidly changing place, where people are sucked into the jet stream of change at warp speed. Without constant attention and commitment to development and growth of its primary resource for attainment of vision, the vision stagnates, and the workers fall along the wayside. For a great leader, today is not good enough, not far enough, not wide enough. A *Legacy* Leader is always thinking in tomorrows. Unless your organization has only a one-day vision, the development of others is absolutely necessary for future success. And this commitment to the development of people to achieve vision becomes an important *value* of the organization.

When John F. Kennedy challenged America's space program to put a man on the moon within the decade of the 1960's, he set a formidable vision. NASA went to work, constantly developing both equipment and personnel to reach the vision. The vision was clear—get to the moon in less than ten years. Current levels of technology, knowledge, skills sets and competencies were not able to meet the vision when the challenge was issued. But development was unceasing, and commitment unwavering. And in less than those ten years that are now in the history books, Neil Armstrong uttered his famous words from the surface of the moon in July 1969. But development didn't stop there. NASA has continued to develop their people and their technology. The vision has changed. Today mankind seeks to walk the plains of the red planet. And the vision will keep changing, and the development will continue. While not all businesses concern themselves with such lofty goals, they all share the same means of achieving them—people. Setting the technology explosion aside, without a similar people development explosion, vision is lost.

A helpful exercise would be to write down the names of your team members and then one or two words after each name that signify the potential you see in each person. Then write at least two practical things *you will do* to encourage that potential. Avoid the temptation to set this list aside. *Do* it. Work at it, add to it, expand it, and achieve it every day.

Consider how this behavior will impact your organization's vision—it's very future—and what would happen *if you didn't* do this.

Sustaining Systems to Achieve Vision and Values

If you are the leader in your area of responsibility, then ultimately it is your job to effectively communicate, then sustain, all the processes and systems of your area in order to achieve the goals of the vision and the core values of the guiding principles.

This assumes your organization already has a set of processes and systems in place to achieve vision and work with values throughout the company. These systems essentially define the way the organization works on a daily basis, and include all processes, responsibilities, accountabilities, expectations and guidelines for behavior and activities. Think about these systems for a moment. Identify and describe them. If you stumble, even slightly, over any one of these areas, then you want to do some serious work here. You cannot communicate something you can't identify or describe. And if you can't communicate them, you certainly can't intentionally sustain them. These are the underpinnings, the gears and engines and levers that run the machinery of your business—they are what will

> You need to know when something is broken....

achieve your vision. They will often require maintenance, and even repair, overhauls and tune-ups. You need to know when something is broken, and the only way you can do that is to have a mechanic's ear and knowledge of how your engine runs. It may even be time for a new model.

Assuming you have this knowledge, it can't stop with you. You not only communicate it, but *teach* it to others. Make your entire work staff diagnosticians and maintenance engineers of all systems and processes. Maintain your business machinery in prime condition, on a daily basis, by communicating and teaching systems and processes, and then sustaining their peak performance through vigilant oversight. Your maintenance specifications include how all processes align with vision and values. A quick word of caution is needed, here, however. Some processes can be more burdensome than they need to be. Allow your routine maintenance to include simplification and optimization, and frequent inspections for natural flow. Streamlining and removal of bottlenecks and unnecessary time and personnel wasters can revitalize an entire organization—and the bottom line.

This Legacy Practice is not merely about having vision and values, but about using them, living them, in daily operations to undergird the entire organization, to reflect the organization's core ideals, and to bring it into a prosperous future. It is what motivates people to do the work of the company and achieve goals. You carry vision and values everywhere you go, protecting, guarding, modeling, never losing sight of them.

From this first practice, the process of legacy building begins. As a leader, consider the parts of yourself that are implanted in others in this environment. What you hold, they hold. Your vision becomes theirs, and your values reside in them.

The Bottom Line

Leadership can be complex. One look at the business section of the local bookstore confirms that. There is no end to leadership competencies, behaviors, skills and practices. For this reason, leadership often takes on a very mysterious quality, where it becomes difficult to grab hold of a pattern or framework for great leadership that stands the test of time. This is the entire concept behind Legacy Leadership—to provide such a framework and structure to build competencies and behaviors that reflect Legacy Leaders and legacy organizations. Like anything else worth pursuing, leadership requires practice. These skills and competencies provide practice points which, when integrated, shape an expert leader. A great pianist learns first to identify the keys, practice the scales, and put harmonious notes together. The point is that every expert, regardless of the field, begins at the beginning, with the basics. Leadership is the same. It begins at the beginning, with the purpose for your existence as a leader, and as an organization. Legacy Practice 1 is this beginning. It is foundational for every other practice, competency or behavior. It lays the cornerstone of your leadership. Everything builds on it, and everything depends on it for perfect alignment. A great building rises only as a result of great plans, and great values, that are intentionally communicated and reinforced throughout the community of construction workers.

Legacy Practice 1 is about direction and commitment. We often refer to this as one of the bookends of leadership, the other being Legacy Practice 5, which is about execution and performance. Without either bookend, the entire shelf of leadership will collapse. If you are intent on becoming a great leader, about *living* (not leaving) your leadership legacy, about building tomorrow's leaders, and about serious success, this is the place to start.

1

Reflection

1. How are you effectively applying, and living, Legacy Practice 1: Holding Vision and Values for leadership legacy?

2. How can you integrate organizational vision and values into your daily tasks for your area of responsibility?

3. What specific areas would you like to develop pertaining to this Legacy Practice?

Next Steps

Do you want to become a student of leadership? Do you wish to shift your leadership from good to great—to living legacy? The Development Guide in the Appendix will help. It contains:

a) The **10 Critical Success Skills:** Core Competencies for Legacy Practice 1

b) **Consideration:** Professional Development *(Questions to guide your development as a Holder of Vision and Values)*

c) **Essence:** Being a Legacy Leader *(The BE-Attitudes of the Holder of Vision and Values)*

d) **Application:** Putting it to Work *(Steps for applying Legacy Practice 1)*

e) **Legacy Shifts:** Expected Outcomes
(Shifts in behavior and environment that can be expected as a result of applying this Legacy Practice)

The Development Guide for Legacy Practice 1 begins on page 203. We encourage you to use this material fully, making the most of opportunities to take your leadership to the next level.

Chapter
TWO

Legacy Practice 2

1
Holder of Vision and Values™

2	3	4
Creator of Collaboration and Innovation™	**Influencer of Inspiration and Leadership**™	**Advocator of Differences and Community**™

5
Calibrator of Responsibility and Accountability™

Real innovation resides within collaboration, which flourishes when opportunities are created rather than awaited.

TWO: Legacy Practice 2

CREATING THE ENVIRONMENT
Creating Collaboration
and Innovation

2

Behind every Academy Award-winning superstar walking the famed red carpet, the bestselling author, and the sports hero signing autographs for adoring fans, is a virtual army of people working tirelessly.

In most cases, without these behind-the-scenes players, our cultural icons would likely exist only as "wanna-be's" still waiting and wishing for elusive stardom. Each one of these heroes and heroines has at least one, sometimes several, people constantly with an ear to the ground and finger in the air, testing the winds and searching for the sounds of opportunity. The work of theatrical, literary and sports agents is to seek and sometimes create opportunities, make connections and bring elements together to catapult their clients to the spotlight. These people are generally well paid, but also usually earn every bit of their compensation. No possibility is overlooked. And where possibilities may not be evident, the agent is adept at creating them. Just check the tabloids at the grocery store. In essence, the agent

As an agent for the success of an organization, the leader constantly seeks opportunity, alert and aware of the winds of potential.

creates connections, which facilitate collaboration, which in the end often results in innovative new paths.

An agent can be described as someone with the power to produce an effect. In the case of cultural icons, that effect is stardom—as an actor, author or sports figure. In the case of the Legacy Leader, the effect is organizational success, and both effects often rely on fresh thinking, new ideas, connections and collaborative innovation. In either case, the work is the same—a vigilant pursuit of possibilities. As an agent for the success of an organization, the leader constantly seeks opportunity, alert and aware of those winds of potential. This Legacy Practice is about not only seeking, but in many cases actually creating, opportunities for collaboration and innovation to thrive and to produce the ultimate desired effect of business success—however that is defined, or envisioned. Just like any other agent, the business leader is alert to possibilities, creates opportunities and encourages collaboration which most often produces innovation. These things don't happen by themselves. The Legacy Leader is an agent, a *creator* of collaboration and innovation.

The leader will create an environment for collaboration and innovation by gathering people with differing perspectives, talents, gifts, and attitudes for the purpose of creating something bigger, better and more significant than any one of them could have done alone. For this leader, the goal is to allow collaboration and innovation to become practiced disciplines within the organization. The created environment is based on the organization's cultural values and vision, as discussed in Legacy Practice 1, and designed to provide opportunity for collaborative innovation.

Leaders challenge current thinking and assumptions, encourage the creation and implementation of better ways and ideas, and role-model for the team or community imaginative and inventive visualization beyond the present reality. Innovation is most often the product of creative collaboration. The Legacy Leader encourages, promotes and protects collaborative innovation through a variety of creative means. The leader continues this process until collaborative innovation is a norm (discipline) of the organizational culture, and is foundational to all attitudes and activities. A Legacy Leader will also keep in mind the selfless basis of collaboration. It is a concept that requires working together to achieve common goals instead of personal agendas. It cannot be done in a vacuum, and cannot be achieved with selfish intention. Trust is the central issue of this Legacy Practice.

> The *Legacy Leader* becomes an active "opportunity seeker" and possibility thinker.

Collaboration and innovation are not automatic functions. They are to be encouraged, nurtured—with opportunities created by leaders. This is not about being creative, it is about being a *creator*, one who instinctively creates opportunities and the environment where collaboration and innovation can flourish. A creator, just like the agent, actually causes something to come into being, in this case collaboration and innovation, sometimes through inventive means. The Legacy Leader becomes an active "opportunity seeker" and possibility thinker. He or she imparts the idea that all players and all ideas are of great value to the whole, and have great contribution to the whole organization's success. This is an attitude of leadership, not just a leadership action.

The incredible successful rise of Whole Foods Market is due in large part to their "Declaration of *Inter*dependence." They have clearly stated a desire, and constantly create the environment, for collaborative innovation among every stakeholder. This is a company-wide mission, and a company-wide attitude. For the past ten years, Whole Foods Market has been named to the *Fortune* magazine list of "100 Best Companies to Work For." Why? Each person is valued, and each person contributes to the collaborative innovation that continues to move the company into successful tomorrows. Whole Foods Market acknowledges it is because they have *created* an empowering workplace where such collaboration and innovation can happen.

People seem to think that successful innovation is mostly a matter of luck—that innovation sinks or swims based on random ideas of random people. While this may actually happen on occasion, it is a fluke, and generally won't happen again. Like lightning, random, unintentional innovation rarely strikes again in the same place. Innovation is a process managed by the leader who creatively and intentionally seeks opportunities and builds an environment where both collaboration and innovation can thrive. We could throw a lot of time-worn adages at you here, like "two heads are better than one," or "it takes a village," but you get the idea. It's not about adages, or what's trendy in leadership these days, but rather about attitude and anticipation—and a creative effort to promote them.

Creating Innovative and Sound Possibilities

> Thoughtful consideration of what is possible, and plausible, lays the foundation for innovative leaps.

Anyone can come up with an idea. We've all had those light bulbs in the shower, but how often do these ideas make it beyond the shower curtain? This practice is about *possibilities*, not just ideas. Possibilities take ideas to the next level, where they become innovative opportunities. The future of any organization is all about innovation. In fact, the future depends on innovation. Before breakthrough innovation occurs, however, thoughtful consideration of what is possible, and plausible, lays the foundation for innovative leaps. And this practice is not just about thinking up new things or being innovative. It is about creating the opportunities for such innovation. Innovation needs to be incubated before hatching.

Before ideas can become real possibilities and opportunities, they should first pass the feasibility and practicality tests. Are they "sound"— logical, plausible, practical? Poor Icarus *(Greek mythology)* had a great idea, but didn't conduct a feasibility study before flying too close to the sun with wax wings. Not only did his attempt fail, but any hope of becoming an idea man like his dad, Daedalus, came to a sudden end. Consider your process to determine if ideas should become possibilities—if they are truly innovative and sound for your organization. Take a full 360-degree turn around yourself, side-to-side, up-and-down, to fully understand how ideas, possibilities and innovation will affect your organization.

In today's business and marketing culture there is a frenzy to find the next best thing, the next new and different idea. King Solomon made a very wise observation in his later years, writing *"there is nothing new under the sun."* Our culture seems determined to prove him wrong. What we often consider "new" is just repackaging, reformatting and reinventing. Sound innovation does not concern itself with repackaging, but rather those things that will take individuals and whole organizations forward on solid ground, not trendy advertising and unmet customer, consumer, client or stakeholder expectations. Reformatting or reinventing will probably not lead to true innovation, yet refinement can. Be sure your ideas and possibility thinking will lead to solid growth, not frivolous expense of time, finances and personnel.

The Incubation
of Innovation

The Legacy Leader creates a learning, trusting environment where true
collaboration and innovation are born. Sounds good, doesn't it? But how
do you do it? Creating an environment of trust is the first and greatest step
toward true collaboration and innovation. Trust is a rare commodity in
today's business world. Unfortunate, but true. So who can begin this nearly
impossible task? Don't look around you; look in the mirror. Regardless of
your position within an organization, you can begin the process of building
a trusting environment—for many purposes, including collaboration and
innovation. This starts with giving people a common sense of purpose, and
making sure that everyone understands the vision, and why you are working
together. Get to know the people around you, facilitate conversations and
build what has become known as social capital. In short, social capital is
the advantage of being connected to others by cultivating networks that
go beyond just bridges to bonds. These connections enable trust, but only
if trust is displayed in return. It is not just about enlarging your circle, but
more about encouraging relationships. Your expanding social capital, when
based on mutual trust, will enable a broader base for innovation through
collaboration. It is impossible to play a baseball game alone. But with a
team of like-minded, skilled and trusting people, you can win the World
Series.

> A multi-billion dollar international agri-business firm
> hired a consultancy to evaluate the company.

The results revealed the company was healthy for the most part, but because
of its far-flung and growing presence around the globe there was very little if

any collaboration among the officers in various geographical locations, and company divisions. Each officer was acting as the head of his or her own company, with little thought to the overall needs of the organization.

Through an intensive executive coaching initiative, the officers of the organization have now developed a process to encourage collaboration, to learn from each other, invest in each other and anchor as a team. They are actively seeking collaborative opportunities, building trust (rather than protecting turf), capitalizing on their varied knowledge and skills and planning more innovatively for the future. These officers still deliver on huge goals for each independent area or division, but they are doing it together, without boundaries, drawing upon the rich resources of the company as a whole. This was not an easy process, but this new environment of trust was fostered with fierce and intentional commitment to a healthier future. It is amazing to watch how innovation grows when trust and collaboration tear down walls.

Innovation leaps ahead when trust and collaboration tear down walls.

Remembering that this Legacy Practice is more about *creating* the environment for collaboration and innovation, a Legacy Leader carefully considers what promotes these—what makes them happen. Structure, encouragement, trust and team attitude are just a few. You have most likely already noticed what conditions allow first collaboration, and then innovation, to occur in your area of responsibility. Pay attention to what these conditions are, and foster that environment. Determine also the conditions that *prevent* collaboration and innovation. Distrust, silo and solo orientation rather than a team approach will severely inhibit any innovation and definitely retard collaboration. If these exist in your organization, consider how you can turn your creative music from solos into full choruses.

While all of the things we've mentioned so far are excellent contributors to the presence of real collaboration and innovation, quite often *you*, as the leader, need to encourage collaboration and innovation by making opportunities for both to be unleashed. You provide the form and structure, as well as the freedom and environment, for collaboration and innovation. How do you do this? Get serious about it. List at least three concrete ways you create opportunity for collaboration and encourage it on a day-to-day basis. Put your list to work for you and *do* it—before it is set aside on your desk to collect the dust of non-collaborative time and missed opportunities.

Specific Ways I Can Create Opportunities for Collaboration	
1	
2	
3	

A Legacy Leader knows how to create the opportunity and structure, and facilitate interaction that contributes to organization-wide success. This kind of leader does not "hold court" in group or team discussions. He or she facilitates conversations by setting the tone and inviting high-quality collaboration. This leader will look for opportunities to create connections between people, which in turn create the opportunity for innovation and collaboration. These connections may be those found in the normal team meeting, or they may be unexpected, arising from an openness to honestly hear everyone's best thinking—including the janitor or the employee in the mail room or cafeteria. The leader who facilitates conversations makes the connections, plugs them in and lets them run—just like the theatrical agent. There are no circuit breakers or limit switches. The leader is primarily a structural conduit for the electricity. Without artful facilitation, however, the electricity can run amok and overload the system.

Facilitating conversations and dialogue is only part of this equation. It isn't always difficult to get people talking. However, getting them to share their best requires real leadership influence. Consider what consistently motivates others to contribute their *best thinking*. List at least five elements that you believe result in the best of innovative and collaborative thinking— elements you can use as "facilitating" attitudes or actions. Put them in play to test your thinking.

Wherever and whenever you find people consistently contributing their best, either in thinking or doing, you will find a Legacy Leader masterfully facilitating conversations and creating environments where true collaboration thrives. The resulting innovation allows the organization, and the individual, to leap ahead toward successful outcomes.

Reviving the Lost Arts of Listening and Questioning

Social capital, our people resource network, does not grow by itself. It requires building relationships, showing worth and value, and displaying empathy. And good relationships require listening well. A Legacy Leader becomes a masterful listener, and a masterful listener provides a safe place for sharing—critical to collaboration. Being a good listener is a learned skill. It's a matter of discipline and *desire* to hear others. That is where listening masterfully really begins—in truly wanting to understand and hear those around you. One of the greatest needs of the human heart is to be *heard*— really listened to. This need does not change in the business environment. The real issue for the masterful listener is humility, and acknowledging that others need and deserve to be heard. Honestly listening, giving your whole attention (not just a token ear in passing) to another person means putting your own desires and your own needs aside, at least for that moment. It

Desiring to really hear others is a choice.

means you truly want to know and understand the other person, to really hear them. To really hear them, you give them your full attention. Have you ever had a conversation with someone who seemed more interested in what he or she would say next, than in listening to what you had to say? Didn't feel very good, did it? Desiring to really hear others is a choice that requires discipline to shut off the voices and distractions inside us and make an intentional *choice* to listen well.

A real listener listens and *hears* both what is spoken, and what is left unspoken. Quite often we learn more from what is *not* said, than from what the person actually voices. The Cable News Network's (CNN) Larry King (*The Larry King Live Show*) is an expert at this. During his interviews, Mr. King asks strategic questions, then settles back to listen well, instead of talking over his guests. When we fill up the airwaves with our own talk, we don't learn a thing, do we? And Mr. King only knows what questions to pose by listening mostly for what is unsaid during his interviews. Become an expert at hearing, or observing, what is not audible. Be a discerning listener, and ask meaningful questions to determine what is not being said.

Locate yourself on this listening scale. Give serious thought to a plan for improvement and commit to sliding your rating on this scale all the way to the right. Remember that listening is learning and knowing, and a crucial step in creating collaboration.

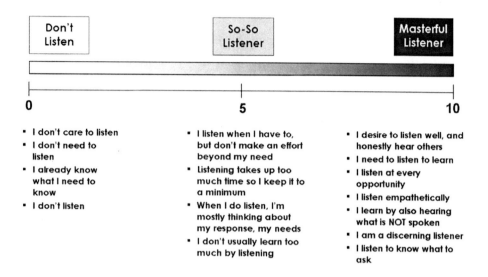

Don't Listen	So-So Listener	Masterful Listener

0   5   10

- I don't care to listen
- I don't need to listen
- I already know what I need to know
- I don't listen

- I listen when I have to, but don't make an effort beyond my need
- Listening takes up too much time so I keep it to a minimum
- When I do listen, I'm mostly thinking about my response, my needs
- I don't usually learn too much by listening

- I desire to listen well, and honestly hear others
- I need to listen to learn
- I listen at every opportunity
- I listen empathetically
- I learn by also hearing what is NOT spoken
- I am a discerning listener
- I listen to know what to ask

Leaders are expected to always have the "big picture" in mind. This is critical to any leadership. "Keeping in mind the big picture" is a nice little phrase we throw around easily. But in reality, it is anything but easy. This basically involves holding vision and values, Legacy Practice 1, but also implies knowing the "big things" while doing the "small things." Strategic planning can provide a road map for these tasks, but within the boundaries of the strategic plan will come the need for countless "collaborative conversations" to measure and mark your direction and action at any given point along the path. And the nature of these collaborative conversations includes another lost art—*asking timely and tough questions.* The ability to artfully craft and ask appropriate questions, when paired with keeping in mind the big picture, becomes a powerful process diagnostic through collaborative, and often innovative, conversation.

Inquiry and questioning are finally experiencing resurgence among those who understand the requirements of great leaders. For the longest time we shied away from questioning, as if it were not polite, or somehow threatening. Even Thomas Jefferson stated once that questioning was not the "mode of conversation" among gentlemen. We disagree. Times have changed, and so has the need to obtain timely information to ensure the future. The successful leader cannot shy away from asking the questions that can yield the correct process for accomplishing vision and goals—even if those questions are tough to ask. But there is both an *attitude* and an *"altitude"* of questioning that can make, or break, this Legacy Practice.

> There is both an attitude and an "altitude" of questioning that can make, or break, this Legacy Practice.

How these questions are asked may determine what answers you receive, and what impact you have on those questioned. Your *attitude* can be either threatening and intimidating, or collaborative and stimulating. Which attitude would elicit a better response from you? The *altitude* of questioning is about how deep or how high the level of inquiry. For example, it is usually fairly easy to ask, and to answer, questions that deal with the what, when, who and where of something. The deeper questions are often about the why and the how. These are the questions that are most difficult to answer, but can provide the most profound insights, and subsequent results.

We have developed a model to not only ask the tough questions, but the right ones, as well as keeping the big picture in sight. The *Collaborative Conversation Model™* can serve as a template to ensure that the questions will produce answers that lead to actions that take you and your organization where you want to be.

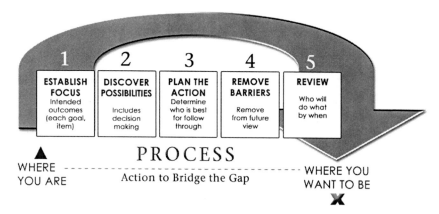

Collaborative Conversation Model™

Try using this template to prepare relevant questions for a "Collaborative Conversation" with your team members. Identify the problem or project you want to move through (WHERE YOU ARE), then ask the hard questions that will provide the process to move you WHERE YOU WANT TO BE. Design your questions to fit within each of these five process areas to bridge the gap. Review your questions to be certain they cover all the needs, possibilities and desired outcomes. This template will help you ask the right questions in a timely manner while encouraging collaborative discussion, and keep the big picture in sight. Remember the *attitude* and *altitude* of questioning. Ask with an attitude that fosters collaboration and innovation, rather than defensive contention. And take the questions to a new altitude, one that doesn't just ask what the outcome will be, but *how* the outcome will serve the organization, and *why* it is desired.

Too often the questions we ask dance all around the heart of an issue. But at that heart are the answers and process for successful execution in business. Dancing doesn't take you anywhere except in circles. If thoughtful questioning is not already practiced, it may make people a bit uncomfortable initially—but these questions draw out learning for everyone. A leader listens, with the bigger picture in mind, in order to ask questions that address the tough issues of the conversation that perhaps no one else would either dare or think to ask. Encourage dialogue and questioning based in reality, even when it might seem uncomfortable or challenging. Be honest, candid and open, and develop a sense of timing that allows you to ask questions and receive answers—before you may have to resort to excuses. The goals are to drive conversations to new levels to reach the best conclusions, and create the environment for the greatest collaboration and innovation. Asking questions creates a more robust conversation and keeps people thinking and discovering new answers. When the answers come, be prepared to listen well.

A Legacy Leader asks appropriate questions with the right attitude and the right ears to listen and hear the answers. It is not just a skill or competency, it is a choice. Intelligent, timely and collaborative questioning can separate a good leader from a great leader, and often a ho-hum organization from a dazzling success story.

No One
Has ALL the Answers

Leaders individually, or teams of leaders collectively, live in what we have termed the *"Zone of Not Knowing."* This zone is an unpredictable place ripe with opportunity, yet extremely uncomfortable for some who believe they need to know everything before they get out on the proverbial limb.

☑ Admit you don't have all the answers.

☑ Become a lifelong learner.

☑ Stay open to ideas and perspectives of others.

Today's business world moves at the speed of light—quite literally—as knowledge is acquired and transactions are made through fiber optic cables that speed information from one side of the globe to the other in seconds. Every day, and sometimes every hour, the business landscape changes, both internally and externally. Leaders who thought they "knew it all" are finding quickly they know *nothing at all* at times. How do you keep up? By admitting you don't have all the answers, becoming a lifelong learner, and being open to the ideas and perspectives of others.

There is much more to learn after you "know it all." And learning quite often comes from surprising sources. If we think of learning as lifelong, realizing we don't have all the answers, we are more prepared to explore the thinking of others to find those answers—in essence creating an environment for collaboration.

Ruth, the vice president of a health care organization, always had to have the "right" answers, and fast.

Over time, this created a situation where Ruth's team members no longer had to think for themselves. They learned to wait for her answers. Her personal need to be the "go to" person created problems for others within her organization. People grew dependent on Ruth, and never engaged in problem solving, since Ruth would always provide the answers. The unique perspectives of her team were never invited. Eventually Ruth began to see that this approach was limiting the growth of her team, and she was beginning to wither under the load of always having to know everything. And good employees were leaving because they didn't feel acknowledged for their contributions. In fact, their contributions weren't encouraged at all. Ruth was a one-woman show, but with an entire team watching, walking through the motions. Ruth had to change her approach—and she did. Today her team is thriving and acknowledged as a top performer in the organization. Ruth relies now on team learning through a collaborative approach—everyone contributes, and everyone grows. When they need answers, they find them together.

Learn to live comfortably in that "zone of not knowing." Use the following chart to rate yourself in these areas.

RATE YOURSELF IN THE FOLLOWING AREAS, on a scale of 1-5, 5 being highest					
How comfortable are you not knowing "the answers?"	1	2	3	4	5
How open are you to learning from others?	1	2	3	4	5
How committed are you to being a learner?	1	2	3	4	5
How often do you seek ideas and perspectives of others?	1	2	3	4	5
Do you listen masterfully to the perspectives of others?	1	2	3	4	5

If you are a Legacy Leader, you will be willing and committed to devising an action plan to bring your answers up to a perfect score. It may take some time, though in fact, practice does make perfect.

So where do you get your answers? Some of them come obviously from research, from experience, and from accessible information through conventional means. By and large, however, most of the leader's answers will come from other people. People carry a wealth of diverse information and knowledge. We are more connected to global conversations and more interested in news around the world. Our expectations have changed from days past—we expect to be involved, to be valued and utilized for our strengths. In essence, we want to contribute our brainpower and offer our wisdom. We are stakeholders with a vested interest in the success of the organization. Commit to making full use of your people resources available to you within your organization. Discover how "borrowed brains" can become some of your richest assets.

Differing Perspectives _____

When we choose to draw out the thoughts and ideas of our fellow workers, we need to be receptive to both the good news and the bad news, including differing perspectives. This is the only way we can be fully informed. Today's leaders need every bit of information and every perspective they can effectively get their hands on. Differing perspectives are the fuel of healthy innovation and productive collaboration. The leader who does not welcome ideas, no matter if they agree or differ with his or hers, will cease to be a leader. It is the leader's responsibility to create the environment where these sometimes differing perspectives and ideas are freely offered and always valued. This environment of freedom of personal expression is built on the acceptance that every human being is unique and of value—and so are their opinions, perspectives and ideas.

> The leader who does not welcome ideas... will cease to be a leader.

Even outright disagreement can lead to some of the best, most productive and innovative collaboration—if it is honored, respected and encouraged. There can be many perspectives of the truth. Giving ear to each of these perspectives increases learning and provides a wider knowledge base for successful decision-making. Ovid, the Roman poet, said, "You can learn from anyone, even your enemy." There is always another perspective beyond your own. The wise leader learns to embrace moments of disagreement as pathways to deeper learning. More learning means more knowledge, which means wiser choices and increased innovation. And what if, just maybe, you were "wrong?"

Following the high-level scandals that screamed from headlines around the world, the Sarbanes-Oxley Act required boards of directors to rethink strategies and oversight.

One nine-member Board of a major insurance company determined they would need to be more responsible than ever with oversight of their C-level leaders, particularly the CEO and CFO. In the process of changing their mode of operation, Steven, the Board Chair, assessed, among many other issues, the status of interaction between the members. In characterizing his findings in feedback to the Board, he stated that one of the main issues he discovered was that Board members were reluctant to offer differing opinions for fear of disturbing the equilibrium of the group. He reported that this prevented them from bringing to the full Board points and perspectives that they might have needed to address. In his words, "we're way too nice to each other, afraid of offending or having any signs of conflict." He added, "Our standard approach keeps us from learning all the things we need to know to make critical decisions to grow the company in the right direction." With the Board's permission, Steven outlined a way they could maintain respect for each other while having full and complete discussions, asking questions and challenging points of view in order to learn from each other. This was not discussion for the sake of debate, but for the sake of educated decision making and collaboration.

Thinking in Tomorrows

Today's leader needs to see into the future, or at the very least be *aware* of the future. It is too easy to become completely focused on yesterday and today, without proper regard for tomorrow. Success, however it is defined, should be an ever-elusive quality. Once an individual or an organization determines they have achieved their goals, forward progress stops cold. Collaboration and innovation are all about the future—about creating opportunities to take individuals, whole organizations, and perhaps even the world, into a better tomorrow. Otherwise, why innovate at all? That better future is reached *through* collaboration and innovation, and both depend on someone creating the opportunities for these components to unite for powerful results. Legacy Leaders are tomorrow thinkers, guiding others into innovative and collaborative futures.

> A Legacy Leader is a practical realist and a visionary idealist—at the same time.

As the pace of change increases, the leader keeps one eye on the present and one eye on the future. It is the leader who holds the vision and sets the tone by bringing the future into the context of the present. The Legacy Leader sees what might be invisible to others, and then translates it and gives it form for his or her team members. The leader becomes the beacon, shining a light into the darkness of the future. With enough light, people become accustomed to what might appear initially to be a dim path, and learn to move forward, in new ways, together. Unless someone holds that light and casts its beam into the future, however, collaboration may collapse, and innovation will die.

As with everything, however, there is a balance to be achieved here. Too much thought and time spent in the future will deprive the present of its own attention. The leader is responsible for this balance in him or herself, as well as in others. A *Legacy* Leader is a practical realist and a visionary idealist—at the same time.

> A century-old multi-billion dollar national insurance company realized that the current way of doing business wouldn't work much longer.

Not in this high-speed, high-tech and changing customer profile world. While maintaining their reputation for excellent customer service, they actively piloted new programs in specific geographical areas, testing and tuning up processes until they were able to be implemented company-wide. Theirs was a winning story illustrating this practice. However, another attempt to leap into tomorrow didn't play out so well in a major national media company. Endeavoring to take the organization into the future, the new head of IT ignored long-standing company culture by outsourcing the majority of their IT. What this highly qualified and capable person forgot, however, were the people behind the technology, and the culture they had created. Turmoil resulted, and without long-term thinking and backup strategy, this organization was thrown into a tailspin, requiring years to recover. The point is, there is a delicate balance between today and tomorrow, people and technology. We innovate *now* for the future, but pay ample attention to the here and now.

> An organization that does not dream *now* about tomorrow, may never make it there.

Any organization that does not dream now about tomorrow, may never make it there. And in today's highly competitive business landscape, innovation is often the difference between organizational survival and extinction. Successful innovation does not happen fully in a vacuum—it requires collaboration and a boost of encouragement. As technology and information continue to explode around us, it is vital to consider what the world will be tomorrow. Anticipated change will drive decision making and without an attitude *and aptitude* for what tomorrow brings, many organizations will become endangered species.

While great leadership needs to innovate now for the future, even this doesn't guarantee success. The really critical factor is the successful *projection* of how these new ideas will be received and "play out" in the organization and the marketplace. Without this, no amount of innovation, or reliance on tried-and-true tactics or strategy, will bring success. This ability, an art in itself, coupled with innovation and collaboration, is what propels individuals and organizations into a successful future. Even if our friend Icarus had performed diligent feasibility studies on the innovative possibility of flying with wax wings, he obviously did not project how his idea would work near a heat source. Projections are to be tied to impact on corporate vision and values. No amount of innovation can ensure that your path to the future will get you where you want to be, or won't lead you and the organization over a cliff. Like Icarus' wax wings, too many great ideas end up in the ocean of failure because of lack of projection. Whether you think this is part of your job responsibility or not, it is. Every leader needs to develop the art of successful projection of ideas.

It is common practice for companies to undertake costly professional feasibility studies before marketing new products or ideas. However, this Legacy Practice is more about common-sense projection. It is about knowing your community, your industry, your organization, and your people well enough to accurately predict how ideas, processes, products and any new concept will work in the real world, not just on paper or in the minds of those imagining such concepts. Is this new idea really innovative? Has it been subjected to the collaborative scrutiny and testing of all the appropriate sounding boards? Have you taken advantage of the available input, the opinions of others, to really test these new ideas? The intent here is that, quite possibly, successful outcomes or potential failures can be determined *before* the need for expensive professional feasibility studies, and before the organization, or the individual, realizes functional failure the hard way.

Change is NOT a Four-Letter Word

Relying on "what works" is generally a good idea. However, stubbornly relying on what worked in the past without regard to the future is a formula for failure. This reveals a lack of innovation and forward thinking. Yet increased collaboration and innovation have a natural side effect: increased change. Are you prepared for this? The need for change is inevitable, especially with this ever-increasing pace of business and global changes. If the external environment changes more than the internal organizational environment, organizational extinction is on the horizon. Just as terminal, however, is change merely for the sake of change. The need for change cannot be determined on a whim, but on practical future thinking and concrete answers to the following questions:

- Why doesn't the old way work anymore? (*What is prompting this change?*)

- What will this change provide for us?
- Does this change support our vision and values, and overall strategy?
- What is this change going to cost *(dollars, people, time, etc.)*?
- Are the costs justified by the benefits of the proposed change?
- What impact will this change have on our "brand?"

Mention the word "change" and people cringe. Change is inevitable, yet largely feared. The human creature naturally resists change. Even if for the better, change often brings discomfort to some. It becomes critical for the leader to be able to assist team members and others to understand when and why change needs to happen—and be just as alert to when it does not need to occur. Communication of vision, research and background information and factors are the keys to getting people onboard for such change. Our resistance to change can be viewed as a survival instinct, until we recognize that the change will be beneficial. Even then, be prepared to ask, and answer, the big questions of *why, when* and *how*. The more information people have regarding impending changes, the better they will adapt and incorporate them. Encourage workers at every level to ask those "need-to-know" questions and be forthcoming with honest answers. Change happens easier when you do it *with* others, not *to* them.

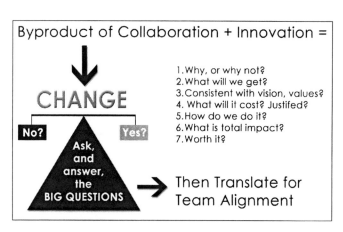

Byproduct of Collaboration + Innovation =

CHANGE

No? Yes?

Ask, and answer, the BIG QUESTIONS

1. Why, or why not?
2. What will we get?
3. Consistent with vision, values?
4. What will it cost? Justifed?
5. How do we do it?
6. What is total impact?
7. Worth it?

Then Translate for Team Alignment

The Bottom Line

Once vision and values are established, strategies are implemented, and a process for preserving and holding these foundations of business (our first Legacy Practice—Holding Vision and Values) is in place, the real work of business begins. This work relies on the creation of collaborative opportunities and innovative ideas (our second Legacy Practice—Creating Collaboration and Innovation) to succeed. But this Legacy Practice is not so much about collaboration and innovation as it is about the *creation of the environment, attitudes and trust* that enable them to happen—and flourish. A Legacy Leader looks for ways to create a collaborative circle among existing teams and structures, puts aside ego and brings out the best in others, opens closed boundaries, encourages continual learning, and generates excitement for shared innovation and the anticipated results. This Legacy Practice is not about simple leadership skills. It is about honest and selfless attitudes of anticipation that create collaborative and innovative competencies in self and others.

Creating Collaboration and Innovation involves an intentional process whereby the environment and culture for collaboration and innovation is created and nurtured. This process respects, honors, affirms and encourages partnership and teamwork. It identifies challenges and sets the ground rules, tears down boundaries, fosters relationships, builds trust and shares everything, including responsibility. And then it develops an attitude of anticipation for the collective and creative future. These competencies will shift individuals and organizations from the ordinary to the extraordinary.

Reflection

1. How are you effectively applying, and living, Legacy Practice 2: Creating Collaboration and Innovation for leadership legacy?

2. How do you encourage your team (as individuals and as a group) to be collaboratively innovative? What is the level of trust in the teams where you participate?

3. What specific areas would you like to develop pertaining to this Legacy Practice?

Next Steps

Do you want to learn how to create environments of trust, and opportunities that enable true collaboration and innovation? Here's what you will find in the Development Guide at the back of this book:

a) The **10 Critical Success Skills:** Core Competencies for Legacy Practice 2

b) **Consideration:** Professional Development *(Questions to guide your development as a Creator of Collaboration and Innovation)*

c) **Essence:** Being a Legacy Leader *(The BE-Attitudes of the Creator of Collaboration and Innovation)*

d) **Application:** Putting it to Work *(Steps for applying Legacy Practice 2)*

e) **Legacy Shifts:** Expected Outcomes
(Shifts in behavior and environment that can be expected as a result of applying this Legacy Practice)

The Development Guide for Legacy Practice 2 begins on page 217. Rather than just reading about creating collaboration and innovation, learn to apply it.

Chapter
THREE

Legacy Practice 3

	1 **Holder of Vision and Values**™	
2 **Creator of Collaboration and Innovation**™	3 **Influencer of Inspiration and Leadership**™	4 **Advocator of Differences and Community**™
	5 **Calibrator of Responsibility and Accountability**™	

If we could look upon the ocean of human behavior, and observe how our every action becomes a drop of radiating influence touching countless other ripples upon that vast sea, we would no doubt be much more intentional about those actions.

THREE: Legacy Practice 3

MOVING PEOPLE FORWARD
Influencing Inspiration
and Leadership

3

Our world is awash in a tidal sea of influencers.
Unless we dwell in a cave or on a
deserted island, we will be repeatedly
influenced, positively and negatively,
all day, every day.

Most people, when considering influence, generally think of what has
come to be called persuasion psychology, or the influencing of the human
masses to do, be or buy something. It's usually about changing minds or
selling ideas and products, a very popular pursuit today, but most definitely
not what this Legacy Practice is about. We are speaking of the human
influencers who shape our being, with their ability to touch hearts and
jump-start self-development and self-motivation to achieve and succeed.

When asked to name the greatest influencers of our time,
people will suggest the icons of the culture, government leaders, media
personalities or others who live in the limelight. While this might be true

on some transient and shallow level, it is usually not true on the deeper, more personal and lasting level. Who were or are the greatest influencers in *your* life? Our guess is you will begin your list with those you've known personally—a parent or other relative, a friend, a teacher, a neighbor, and yes, perhaps even a boss. Generally the greatest influencers in our lives are those with whom we have interacted in everyday life, not those seen from afar and observed through plasma screens.

Legacy Practice 3 is the heart of Legacy Leadership. It is all about relationships, and connecting with those around us to influence, inspire and lead them into their own place of greatness. It is about being and providing intentional inspiration, constant influencers to mold and shape the core of the future generation of leaders—doing today's work in a way that builds tomorrow's workers.

For every pilot who has experienced the thrill and freedom of soaring through the skies, there is at least one great earthborn relationship critical to flight—that of pilot and instructor. Well before he or she takes to the air, the instructor teaches a novice pilot the skills and competencies needed to fly an airplane—all the knobs and dials and nuances of the craft as well as those of the pilot. After instruction comes demonstration, and then practice. During these early lessons, the instructor accompanies the new pilot in the air, practicing takeoffs and landings, figure-eights and other established exercises, building and fine-tuning the learner's skills, and allowing plenty of opportunity for the new pilot to put the lessons to work. Unlike eagles who push their young out of the nest, the instructor takes the student through a consistent series of practice maneuvers that eventually leads to solo flights, but only after much education, encouragement and experience.

Long before this flight of independence, the instructor has thoroughly demonstrated what it really means to take the controls of a flying machine. The student pilot has observed not only *what* the instructor does, but *how* he does it, cataloguing for future reference reactions to bad weather, a sputtering engine, a sudden cross wind, or a down draft leading to a frightening fall from level flight. Every moment of instruction, from academics to aerial problem-solving, influences what kind of pilot this student becomes, and how he or she will handle the unpredictable winds of flight. There are many stories of experienced pilots who have encountered incredible circumstances that *could* have been tragic, had they not been influenced by the actions, and attitudes, of former instructors. A good flight instructor establishes a unique connection with the student on a head *and heart* level that influences and inspires for years and experiences to come.

> Great leaders understand that whether they intend it or not, their performances are observed— admired and copied... or rejected.

A great leader is such a flight instructor, one who not only teaches but demonstrates his or her years of flying the business skies. If this leader is in direct relationship with others, the flying lessons include serious practice exercises. And when you're in the air, all relationships are built on trust and the genuine concern for the well-being of others.

Great leaders understand that, whether they intend it or not, their performances are observed—admired and copied, or rejected. Either way, they are influencers. *Everyone* is. The broad reach of human influence is dramatically seen through a little exercise we use to illustrate this concept. We ask people to draw what looks like an organizational chart, with them at the top of the chart, or at the center of a growing circle. From this chart's center or top, they are to draw boxes for each person they touch, both professionally and personally—as many as they can think of. These boxes are connected with lines to the center, or top of the chart representing that person. They are to then indicate, in the same fashion, all the people that *these* people touch—as many as they have knowledge of—and on and on as far out as they can take the chart. This includes family, friends, community networks, business relationships, and other connections—and the connections of those connections. We then stand back and watch as the dawning of understanding is reflected in both the drawings and the faces of those beginning to fully grasp the importance of influence.

What becomes spectacularly evident is that we influence others much more than we initially thought. Most people who begin these charts either "scrunch" up their diagrams or use additional paper, as their circle of influence continues to grow and grow beyond the boundaries of their original thinking. The picture of a single drop of water impacting the surface of a lake with growing rings of "influence" is not enough to fully illustrate the real concept of influencing others. You would somehow have to use many other rings of droplets, all intersecting and spreading influence, to begin to understand this. The real point here is that you influence others more than you think, and that influence spreads and spreads and spreads, to places and people you may have no knowledge of. It is well beyond our ability to conceive.

> Whether we like it or not, whether we plan it or not, we all influence others.

And for this reason, the Legacy Leader understands the scope of his or her influence, in order to be a truly intentional influencer. You *will* influence—there is no choice in that. But you can choose *how* you influence.

The Legacy Leader will influence in many ways, but we have singled out *inspiration* and *leadership* as the main areas concerning a leader who wishes to build legacy for future leaders. Influencing *inspiration* is about affecting how a person is inspired, inspires others, and produces inspired work. Influencing *leadership* is about shaping and molding the leadership qualities and competencies of other people. One of the biggest aims of a Legacy Leader is to build the future generation of inspired and competent Legacy Leaders—the next generation of influencers.

Dynamic Influence

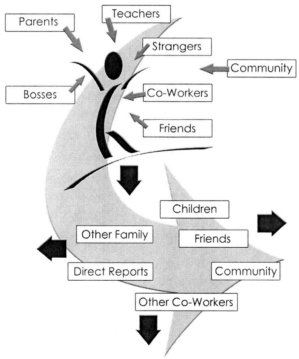

It never ends.
A ripple can become a tidal wave.

You may wish to chart your own influence like the exercise above (*it's quite an eye-opener*), but for now, consider the people who have influenced you most, and their characteristics and behaviors that impacted you. These people may not necessarily be business associates. They may include teachers, parents, friends or even strangers. Whether you know it or not, their influence in your life has had lasting effect on your leadership—on who you are.

> *Whether* we influence is not in question. *How* we influence is.

Whether we are aware of it or not, whether we plan it or not, we all influence others. *Whether* we influence is not in question. *How* we influence is. A Legacy Leader understands that we cannot *not* influence, and therefore becomes an intentional influencer—for good. An *influencer* brings about a desired positive effect in others, either by direct or indirect means. It is about having a consciousness that all that we do influences, even when we aren't aware of it, either in a positive way, or a negative way. The Legacy Leader makes a choice to be an influencer in a positive manner, regardless of the situation or circumstances, in the big things and in the little things. This becomes a way of life, a way of being. This awareness tempers and guides our behavior both personally and professionally.

Inspiration is the process of animating and encouraging others to reach new levels of achievement. The Legacy Leader will influence inspiration by creating an environment that brings people to life and fills others with energy. In doing so, others will then bring inspiration and life to the organization. *Leadership*, simply, is the process of guiding and directing others to shared success. In this Legacy Practice, it is about both personal leadership development and the influencing of sound leadership in others. This influencing leader is a strong proponent of his or her own personal development, as well as the development of others, never satisfied to remain at status quo. The Legacy Leader will influence the leadership of others by leading through positive rather than negative influence, and by encouraging the discovery and development of positive leadership styles in others.

Legacy Practice 3 is about growing, promoting and sustaining inspirational leadership by always providing a consistent and positive role model, by creating opportunities for learning and growing of personal leadership styles and encouraging ongoing and lasting positive energy and passion in others.

> ## Motivation lights a fire, but inspiration is the wind that keeps it roaring.

This is *not* about motivation. Influential inspiration goes well beyond motivation. A leader cannot motivate someone else, but can inspire others to motivate themselves. It transcends short-term "pumping up" for an unsustained burst of energy. There is a grand chasm between generated attitude and genuine inspiration. Influential inspiration is connecting with others personally and deeply, revealing and developing their strengths, using anecdotal stories that genuinely inspire and understanding what does and does not inspire others. This kind of inspiration empowers. Motivation lights a fire, but inspiration is the wind that keeps it roaring. The intentional influencing of inspiration is a consistent path of positive and passionate role modeling.

This kind of leader is selfless, placing the growth and development and achievement of others even before his or her own. This is not just a skill or competency, it is an attitude, a foundational personal and professional precept that drives the Legacy Leader. These leaders are not looking to clone others just like themselves, to be politically correct by speaking a certain language of inspiration, or indulge in kingdom- or empire-building. They genuinely care for and choose to influence others to their own heights of inspiration and leadership achievement. And along the way a strange thing happens. The leader, the organization, and the people grow.

Mary Kathlyn Wagner was a country girl from Texas who enjoyed moderate success in direct sales for about 30 years from the 1930s until the early sixties. She retired in 1963—for about an hour. Her sales experience left her frustrated over the opportunities for women in business, so she decided to write a book that evolved into the beginnings of a business empire. Today Mary Kay® Cosmetics includes a product line of over 200 premium products, 800,000 independent consultants in 37 countries on five continents, over $2 billion in sales, and a rich legacy of charitable activity. This business, frequently hailed as one of the most successful enterprises ever, was not a fluke. It didn't happen because the world needed more cosmetics. It happened because one leader cared about others, and set out to do something about it. Mary Kay's initial goal was to enrich others and she began by making genuine, individual connections of the heart. Her founding principle was the Golden Rule, and she was consistently supportive and enthusiastic about others. She increased her business one relationship at a time and the multiplication factor of intentional influence became a spreading network of other caring and inspiring leaders. She practiced "praising people to success," and preached a business ethic and philosophy that focused on others. Her commitment to this ethic never wavered, and her success has given rise to the success of countless others. Mary Kay's mission of working with a spirit of caring, and living values, is present even after her death in 2001, as Mary Kay Cosmetics continues to grow. Her business philosophy has even been cited in courses at Harvard Business School. Mary Kathlyn Wagner became an intentionally positive influential leader—in the biggest way. So can you.

Building and Maintaining Relationships

If this practice is the heart of Legacy Leadership, then building solid relationships is the heart of this practice. The distinguishing mark of a great leader is the importance they place on personal relationships. Obviously, a certain level of relationship is necessary in order to function properly in business. However, the Legacy Leader goes beyond the minimum standards for relationships to the realm of genuine caring and real knowledge about team members. Great leaders honestly care about both the personal and organizational success of those they lead, and know how to show this concern in appropriate ways. These leaders understand their team members, truly know them, their abilities and their challenges. When people feel that they are understood, they are far more likely to be open to influence.

> Legacy Leaders desire the success of those they lead.

Legacy Leaders desire the success of those around them—those they lead. They actively seek to build more leaders. A leader caring about individuals, however, is only one part of developing and maintaining relationships. In business, individuals come together to form a collaborative and productive team. The leader influences others to build relationships and for entire teams to develop working relationships with one another. Some people see relationships as a "soft" side of business. In reality, it needs to be considered just as important, if not more so, than all the individual tasks, functions and strategies of business. The amount of time you spend investing in relationship building, and encouraging it in others, will eventually determine the character and ultimate results of your leadership, and may even make or break the success of your organization.

Sometimes it is not enough just to be able to develop relationships. It is vital to ensure that they are a constant priority, and can be maintained even when you are not personally involved.

A few years ago a large government agency reorganized itself to bring several new branches into each region.

The merger revealed huge differences in standards and processes, in relationships among employees and agencies, and real gaps between old field and new merged field offices. Max, the senior comptroller, was well known for his relationship building skills, but with the influx of many more branches and people he recognized that he could not physically build and maintain these needed new relationships. Through a one-year plan, Max visited all the new branches to establish new relationships, as well as maintain all the pre-existing ones. He developed a thoughtful strategy of bringing the new agencies and their employees together with his old team, and began a cross-educational process of best practices. Instead of making the gaps wrong or negative, he looked for places to recognize good work, while simultaneously raising the bar on team expectations. The process generically improved the best practices across the entire region, and began the collaboration and communication between newly acquired branches and the previous historical regional branches.

This greatly enlarged region, however, was now too large for Max to personally see and know all the employees, as he had before. Knowing the importance of these continued relationships, Max planned quarterly events with subjects of interest to everyone, and brought the branches together to continue to give branch managers time with him, so they felt well served and understood. He also very intentionally selected several of his most senior people and began to coach them on how to build and maintain relationships. These people had been hired for their technical abilities, yet he put just as much emphasis on the technology of human interaction, training and coaching this senior team to fill in the gaps where he was no longer available. This key team was out in the branches, modeling the environment and culture that the senior comptroller was so well known for personally. At the end of the year he had merged all the branches and people into one functional group that had built relationships with each other and felt valued and respected. The work output was of a higher level than anyone expected, and higher than any of the others where similar mergers had occurred. Max's focus on relationship-building is now being implemented in other regions. He was recognized at the highest levels for his ability to create and maximize very effective long-term relationships as a major strategy for getting the work done.

Keeping it Positive

Leadership is all about choices, and our attitude of leadership and foundational perspective is one of the biggest choices of all. We *choose* whether we model the negative, or the positive, in all situations. This does not mean that you avoid being realistic. Being positive means that you are truthful, and that your message is delivered in a way that is respectfully given and heard. A *Legacy* Leader chooses to model the positive perspective at *all* times. The way you think, positively or negatively, shapes your potential for well-being, personally, professionally and organizationally.

> The way you think, positively or negatively, shapes your potential for well-being, personally, professionally and organizationally.

Three mega-corporations set up a company whose only function was to handle the claims submitted against a product that these three organizations had manufactured years ago.

These claims involved health, safety and legal issues regarding class action suits on a national level. The company was to have a set terminus of approximately ten years, by which time all claims were supposed to be settled. From the start this newly formed company began its life on all negative terms. All of the calls coming in would be negative, even angry. There was no plan for growth for this company, so all employees would consider these dead-end jobs. The work they were to do was unpleasant. Paul, the vice president of this new company, realized quickly that such an environment and culture of negatives would eventually produce very negative work results and negatively thinking and acting employees. Paul decided he wouldn't let that happen, and was determined to establish a culture of fun, relationship building, and positive employee benefits. He instituted innovative call centers where fun was the by-word. This didn't mean work was not professional. It merely meant the people could have fun and keep their spirits high, positive, and better able to meet the needs of angry people. Wherever possible, Paul counteracted this potentially negative environment with positives, like flexible work hours, offsite leadership training, relationship building events, leadership development courses for anyone who wanted them, and excellent severance packages. He worked with the Board of Directors to do everything he could for the employees, developing them into better-trained and better-qualified employees for whatever positions they found after this company was closed. Even now, as the company is downsizing and preparing for its end, Paul is seeking partnerships with others to perhaps make this company into a bigger and sustainable organization to handle multiple class action suits and guarantee more employee stability and mutual benefits. Through it all, Paul has maintained a selfless, positive leadership model, and has built safeguards in to protect others from the negative impacts of such a company, while still expecting the highest quality of work. His employees are treated in a positive way, and they work positively in return.

> The concept of a leader's *warmth* is linked to leadership effectiveness.

When viewed from an emotional standpoint, the word "negative" (and the attitude) tends to leave us cold and dark—repelled. In contrast, the word "positive" (and a positive attitude) connotes warmth and light—attraction. On many leadership assessments the participant is asked to rate a leader or boss on his or her "warmth." What we call *warmth* is firmly linked to leadership effectiveness. Warmth alone won't make a successful and effective leader, but it is a strong factor. A truly effective leader is competent, and one whose employees consider *warm*.

Emotional Intelligence (EI) is a hot topic in the business world. It is a term that has been used for some time now to relate to a person's both innate and developed abilities in the areas of self-awareness (particularly as it applies to personal emotions), self-confidence, self-control, self-motivation and people skills such as empathy, understanding others, influence, conflict management, etc. There is a wealth of information readily available on Emotional Intelligence, so we won't pursue that course here. However, a great leader is aware that Emotional Intelligence and positive energy play a huge role in the success of individual employees and entire organizations, and it all begins with the leader. His or her mood, behaviors, attitudes and energy will not only affect, but quite possibly even drive, those of everyone else in the organization. Since everyone watches the leader, moods, emotions, attitudes and energy spread like a fire out of control—a fire that can either drive the entire engine forward with great passion and energy, or consume and destroy it.

In the late 1990s cities all across the southern United States faced a crisis.

For decades the south was the busy hub of textile production for clothing manufacturers. With the advent of the North American Free Trade Agreement (NAFTA), however, these southern-based textile plants suffered from an increasing migration to Canada and Mexico for finished goods. One by one, like a staggered line of dominoes, the plants closed their doors. In a small rural town of Georgia the workers at one textile plant that had been the main economic force keeping this town afloat came to work one day to find the doors chained and padlocked. The new owners had defaulted on their loan, abandoning the plant and the people. This little town was facing serious economic depression, if not extinction.

But the president and general manager of the mill was not content to leave it at that. He realized the impact this closure would have all over town. The very existence of this formerly healthy and thriving community was at risk. The only other place these workers could find employment in their industry was 100 miles away. So this former president decided he would find a way. His efforts were tireless, and his energy was contagious. Soon the town leaders were on the bandwagon to save the mill and the workers' jobs. They didn't know how they would do it, they just continued as if they would.

Throughout this journey, the former head of the mill generated positive energy and enthusiasm, gaining not only town support but regional, state and federal support. This story has many twists and turns, but just a short two months after the mill closed, with the help of a federal loan, the plant re-opened its doors, having now become a cooperative solely owned by the employees themselves. Wise decision making and operational spending (they even brought their own toilet paper from home in the beginning) coupled with pride of ownership, turned a chained plant into a once-again thriving resource in this small rural Georgia town. None of it would have happened without the emotional intelligence, diligence and positive energy of one man, who influenced others, who then influenced others. It begins with one, who makes an emotional connection with another. This kind of influence starts with one drop in the lake, but becomes ripple upon ripple upon ripple, eventually reaching the shore.

Not all of our ventures, journeys, projects or tasks will have such important impact, but great things often start small, and are fanned into existence by the energy we contribute, and the empathy and attitude we exhibit—for both projects and people. Our emotional intelligence and positive energy influence the people who produce the projects. People are the driving force of any enterprise. Without the ability to positively influence them, we cannot expect to achieve desired results.

> One definition of positive energy in leadership is the attitude of working from intent of success rather than fear of failure.

We are assuming that you are well aware of the concept of Emotional Intelligence, and even beyond that, are aware of your own. This practice does not seek to assess your EI. The intent is to make you aware of its use as an influencer within leadership. Even though we are probably born with certain EI tendencies, we can work to change and improve the ones that impact us and others negatively. The term "positive energy" is linked strongly with EI, but it is also a more comprehensive term that relates to your overall attitude of leadership. One definition of positive energy in leadership is the attitude of working from intent of success rather than fear of failure.

Minimizing the Negatives of Tough Decisions

Tough decisions often mean some negative impact. This competency is about minimizing the negatives and emphasizing the positives, especially as they affect your team members and the organization as a whole. Situations requiring tough decisions may include adversity or obstacles, which can seem to overpower the potential positives. The Legacy Leader keeps negative impact to a minimum, and models behavior that enhances learning and opens doors to opportunity for future success. The focus here is not so much on making tough decisions. There will always be tough decisions to make. It is about ensuring positive, not negative, attitudes and impacts and influencing others to see the greater good. It is part of our human nature to first see the negatives of anything, especially change and risk, which the human creature attempts to avoid like the Black Death. Often buried just below the negative surface, however, are the positive jewels. It is a rare leader who can expose this treasure for others to see and embrace. This is a cultivated skill, and a necessity for the leader who aspires to success—and legacy. Exposing the positive, and adapting to it, opens the doors of possibility. We humans are also pretty good at adaptation, but we need someone holding the light to show the way. Even in adversity there is potential good, and unlimited possibilities for growth. The Legacy Leader knows how to discover these potentials and translate them for others to embrace.

When tough decisions mean change, the Legacy Leader lessens the negatives of change, and points out the positive. Marcus Aurelius was one of the so-called "Five Good Emperors" of the Roman Empire at the height of Rome's prosperity in the second century, and something of a philosopher. One of his philosophical tidbits has great merit and deserves some thought here: *"Is your cucumber bitter? Throw it away. Are there briars in your path? Turn aside. That is enough. Do not go on and say, 'Why were things of this sort ever brought into the world?'"*

Many people say they learn leadership from their bosses—the good ones to copy, and the bad ones to avoid. We've all heard the expression "I'd go to the wall for this person." When you make a tough choice, would you say your co-workers might emulate your style—or avoid it? Will they "go to the wall" for you?

Bring out the Best, then Acknowledge It _____

"Bring out the best in people" is a seemingly simple statement that defies description. Just exactly how do we bring out the best in others? How has the best been brought out in you? Doing this is not easily elaborated and varies from leader to leader, and team member to team member. There are some commonalities, however, and one of those is to always *encourage* and *expect* the best. We recall an old story that makes a solid point here.

> Steven, a bright but underachieving student, went through year after year of failing performances, still managing somehow to be passed on to the next grade level.

At each new grade teachers would try their best to elicit the kind of effort they knew Steven was capable of. Nothing worked, not even threats and public derision. He refused to do any homework, and merely filled a chair during class time. One teacher, however, refused to give up. She discovered that Steven came from an alcoholic home, and spent most of his time holed up in the woods outside his filthy house. This teacher knew Steven had potential, but her efforts went unheeded. She tried talking with Steven, even telling him in front of the class that he was the brightest there, yet failing. Nothing. Finally one day, in her frustration, she blurted out, "Steven, don't you know I care about you?" Suddenly, a small light pierced the dark curtain of despair in Steven's heart and mind. No one had ever told him that before. No one had ever shown him that before. That day after class he grabbed his customary peanut butter and crackers and headed out to his safe haven in the woods, armed with the day's homework. The next morning he proudly handed in the homework and the teacher was stunned. From that day on, Steven continued to work hard and excelled in everything he did. He went on to become a decorated and distinguished Navy officer, and later an influential business leader. The key to Steven's performance? Someone cared, and showed it. When people know their leaders care for them, they are more likely to offer their best.

> **When people know their leaders care for them, they are more likely to offer their best.**

Let's get serious and practical. List ways you can, in general, bring out the best in people you work with. Go ahead, get out the paper now, and write them down (or make notes in this table). List three of your team members. Next to each name, give specific ways you can bring out the best in each of them—as individuals. *Then do it.*

Names	How I can bring out the best in this person
Team Member #1	1.
	2.
	3.
Team Member #2	1.
	2.
	3.
Team Member #3	1.
	2.
	3.

While bringing out the best in people is undeniably a difficult-to-define subject, it most definitely includes inspiring communication. This Legacy Practice is all about *influencing*, and bringing out the best in people includes influencing and inspiring them to do and be their best. We will not attempt to tackle the do's and don'ts of powerful communication, but one of the most rewarding ways to do this is through the artistry and skill of

> # Storytelling in business can be one of the most powerful (and inspiring) communication tools.

storytelling. Storytelling in business can be one of the most powerful (and inspiring) communication tools. Telling someone what to do, or how things are to be, does not have nearly the effect of sharing stories that inspire, teach, motivate or guide. Stories can powerfully convey knowledge because they don't tell—they show. They can dramatically influence and move people to do and know things because they touch a common place in all of us. A Legacy Leader will develop stories from business, and even personal experiences, and use them to evoke the best in others. Great leaders are even willing to share their own mistakes through powerful stories that influence people effectively. It is a good use of your thought time to develop a varied story-telling repertoire. Look for opportunities where you can communicate more effectively by sharing a story, instead of a command or off-hand remark.

Others-Centered

One of the foundations of Legacy Leadership is that it is *others*-centered, instead of self-centered. The focus of a *Legacy* Leader is on building up others, which includes recognizing and acknowledging the attributes and contributions of these people. Each of the words, *acknowledge* and *recognize*, has two different applied meanings here. *Acknowledge* means to admit something as real or true, and to show or express appreciation or gratitude for something or someone. *Recognize* means to identify or become aware of, and to formally reward. Putting it together, there is a sequence of actions that occurs to completely satisfy this competency:

- Consistently looking for the attributes and contributions of others

- Acknowledging that they are real and true, worthwhile and praiseworthy

- Showing or expressing appreciation for them in specific terms

- Formally rewarding them

When Legacy Leaders work to bring out the best in those they lead, they are also prepared to acknowledge and recognize those best efforts. Great leaders have identified the attributes and contributions of team members. They know their team members well enough to look for them, and are *others*-centered enough to actually recognize them. They can admit to real achievement in others, and their worthiness of commendation. You won't fool people, however, into thinking you care—when you don't. They will know the difference. The leader's heart is fully engaged in this process, and has a genuine desire to encourage and inspire others. You can't do this for show only, because the only thing it will show is your hollowness. It takes a true legacy heart. All humans long for acknowledgement, to know they are of genuine value and importance. When a leader honestly says (and shows) "well done," the human spirit can, and usually does, soar to new heights of achievement.

The 3 E's:
Encourage,
Expect, and
Endorse
the best.

Delegate to Develop:
*"Going Self-less"*_____

We all know that a good leader is a good delegator. The intentional delegation that marks a *Legacy* Leader, however, is thoughtful and deliberate, with the specific intent to develop others. Assigning tasks is one thing; developing others through delegation is a hallmark of leadership with legacy. This is what legacy in leadership is all about. Leaders may randomly distribute tasks in order to "get the job done." While this is important, a Legacy Leader knows the attributes and skills of team members and what will challenge them to growth and future success. Delegation becomes a pathway to development. Delegation has its obvious rewards for the leader as well. The more the leader delegates, the easier his or her job becomes. Workers desire challenge, and most will gladly accept new responsibilities, especially projects tailored to their strengths and skills. The leader is still needed for expertise, advice and guidance, but is now not buried under the weight of the task itself.

> Delegation becomes a pathway to development.

Those in leadership positions sometimes fall prey to a serious attitude that severely hampers not only personal growth, but the growth of others. This is the attitude of hoarding or limiting information, power, and the ability for others to experience growth building opportunities—instead of opening the doors to allow everyone to contribute wholly to the success of the organization and experience personal achievement. This leader is like a squirrel, frantically grabbing and storing away nuts for the winter, and then forgetting where he put them. All the things he has hoarded are of no practical use, and his stashing activities are a serious waste of time.

Consider how you can use delegation as a development tool for the advancement of others. One of the most vital elements of successful organizations is self-less leaders in key positions who are committed to the nurturing and development of other leaders at every level of the organization. It is also critical that leaders who build other leaders have an excellent working knowledge of cutting-edge leadership technologies, models, styles and language, and then provide appropriate opportunities to develop the leadership abilities, skills and styles in those they lead. The bottom line of this practice is influencing leadership and inspiring the growth of others. Is your goal to merely "do the job" or is it also to sustain the success of your organization by purposely building future great leaders?

As scandalous headlines continue to tarnish the hallowed halls of corporate leadership, one common denominator among those responsible for this blight on business today is easy to spot— selfishness. The focus and motivation of all their activities is *self*. It is, unfortunately, human nature to desire to elevate self, rather than others. Therefore, it is a conscious choice and a firm commitment to do what is contrary to human tendency—to showcase others. Part of developing and building others is showcasing them, putting them in the spotlight, elevating them, and seeking their success—often before our own.

> One of the most vital elements of successful organizations is self-less leaders in key positions who are committed to the nurturing and development of other leaders at every level of the organization.

Quite often showcasing others is a matter of the heart, rather than the head. If you don't honestly desire to do this, it will be a very difficult task, constantly battling self. Legacy Leaders are not selfish; they desire to share power, share opportunity, and share success. These leaders always look for opportunities to showcase others. The leaders who rise to the top, the ones we grant the title of "great," are generally those who intentionally focus on others. And the opposite is also true. Those people who are self-interested instead of others-interested, usually never make the list of great leaders. This "others-focused" tendency seems so contrary to what we experience in corporate communities today. Does it exist in yours?

> The leaders who rise to the top, the ones we grant the title of "great," are generally those who intentionally focus on others.

In the interest of developing your ability to become an inspiring storyteller, can you think of a brief but powerful story to illustrate these concepts quickly and dramatically? We'll give you an example. Even timeless fables can convey and enhance timeless concepts. Leonardo da Vinci is well known for his inventions, but did you also know he wrote fables? In one short piece called "The Peacock," da Vinci tells of a barnyard of neglected starving animals who can do nothing more than conserve their strength in stillness—all except one, the peacock. Here are the last lines of this fable: *"Mamma," a skinny little chicken asked the hen, "why does the peacock spread his tail every day?" "Because he is vain, my child. And vanity is a vice that disappears only with death."* We'll let you determine the moral to this one.

Arrogance and selfishness in leadership will not win in the end. The self-focused leader has no loyal employee following, no one to protect him or her. Eventually employee performance falls short, goals are not achieved, and success for this leader is elusive. And all the "little people" this leader thought were beneath him or her will merely turn their backs and smile when the selfish leader bites the dust. The highest pinnacle of success often lies in the trust, loyalty and respect of others we have showcased and developed selflessly.

> Arrogance and selfishness in leadership will not win in the end.

Inspiring Through Risk-Taking

This section is not a treatise on the "how-to's" or benefits of risk-taking. Rather, it is about how a true Legacy Leader *models* risk-taking *courageously* in order to inspire others to follow. Obviously, feasibility, practicality and plain old common sense have to be factors in risk-taking. We're talking about informed and intelligent risks, not reckless actions that endanger others or the organization. That kind of foolhardy risk-taking will never inspire anyone to follow—quite the opposite.

The Legacy Leader makes deliberate and well-thought out choices, not only for the advancement of the organization, but also as a mentor who shows the way, inspiring others to have courageous expectations. People will rise up to meet challenges and overcome obstacles when they understand the purpose and value of their efforts, when they have a leader to follow into the relative unknown of change and risk. Risk does involve courage, both to lead and to follow. The Legacy Leader assures those following him or her that the risk is worthy and wise, and that the potential sacrifices are justified.

> For generations an industry-leading agricultural equipment manufacturing company located in the mid-western United States has hired executives with similar profiles due to the nature of its location and its unique kind of business.

In the past few years, however, this organization has, along with all of its competitors, gone global. Even though it branched out with amazing speed and captured much of the available international market, it continued to promote executives with the same profiles and cultural backgrounds. As competition tightened and more markets opened, it soon became apparent that the division and international regional executives, who all shared typically American resumes, would not be sufficient for future growth. This American company had to become culturally diverse, immersed in local culture and led by local people, if it were to survive in the international market. At least that was the firm conviction of one senior executive. In addition to this leadership conundrum, the agricultural division of this organization became so large it had to be split between two senior leaders—Jarod and William. Jarod believed that the company should begin a change in their hiring practices to include leaders from the local cultures, but William did not. Jarod persisted, however, and courageously began a diverse hiring protocol for international positions. He was risking everything, including his own officer-level position. With courage and commitment and long-range vision for competitive advantage, Jarod held fast and not only pursued his "different" hiring practices, but set about educating his board and fellow officers so they too could begin to envision the benefits of this new policy. With time, continued courage and dogged determination, Jarod's risk paid off handsomely. This company is enjoying wide recognition and success in local global markets, due largely to the local leaders influencing their local economies and making local connections.

Without Jarod's courage and inspiring risk-taking, this organizational picture might not have been so bright. His ability to place himself squarely in front of the oncoming train, willing to risk his own position for the good of the organization, served to inspire other leaders to begin questioning old generational policies and procedures and begin streamlining them for the new global business market. Today Jarod and William work together forming cross-functional and cross-platform review teams to evaluate changes and take the needed risks—together—for sustained competitive advantage.

Developing risk-taking skills is one thing. Inspiring others to follow is another. People are much more likely to jump onboard the risk train when they have been included in the decision making, or when they are kept completely informed, and not somewhere in the dark fringes.

> Pride needs to be right, while humility wants only what *is* right.

Humility and Unwavering Resolve

Many seem to think that leadership and humility are oxymoronic. On the contrary, a true leader, a *Legacy* Leader, *must* lead with humility. There is no option. Some people seem to consider leadership as ruling over a kingdom of serfs—slaves to their commands. Command and Control leadership doesn't work anymore, if it ever truly did. Business success today is about team efforts, involved people, and skilled yet humble leadership to guide the process. Albert Einstein eloquently stated: *"The high destiny of the individual is to serve rather than rule."* This is the great leader's motto. While we can "take" pride in our work, being pride-full has no place in leadership. Pride needs to *be* right, while humility wants only what *is* right.

"Unwavering Resolve" is the "10" on the commitment scale of 1 to 10. This is not just a commitment to your work, but a resolve to accomplishing it as a team. It is a resolve to join forces as *one* unit instead of featuring a solo act seeking singular credit. It is your opportunity as a Legacy Leader to build the leaders of tomorrow, while accomplishing the goals of today. This takes unwavering, unflinching resolve.

Lao Tzu, an ancient Chinese philosopher, captured this concept. Consider this:

> To lead people, walk beside them...
> As for the best leaders,
> the people do not notice their existence.
> The next best,
> the people honor and praise.
> The next,
> the people fear;
> And the next,
> the people hate.
> When the best leader's work is done
> the people say,
> 'We did it ourselves!'

Humility can be the luster and shine on the jewel of leadership. It serves to polish competencies and skills and make them more user-friendly, especially in a decidedly unfriendly environment of corporate contest. Unwavering resolve is the commitment to stay the course and inspire others to do the same, while accepting the "costs" of such commitment.

One hazard of leadership success can be its tendency to lull us into a false sense of personal achievement, contributing to a dangerous complacency about our weaknesses and areas of challenge. Without the spirit of humility, we lose sight of all the factors—and people—that contributed to our success. Attaining leadership success is easier than maintaining it. It is short-lived unless we humbly acknowledge that we are not the sole reason for that success. Maintaining leadership strength requires honest personal humility coupled with professional skills and unwavering resolve to attain goals as a team.

The Bottom Line

This Legacy Practice stokes the fires of great leadership. It is what drives and sustains all of what this book, this leadership model, is about. It is about becoming an influential leader who inspires others to greatness. This influential leader, this *Legacy* Leader, knows him- or herself well, is self-inspired, and knows what inspires others. He works to discover the strengths of others to better inspire them, and expresses a positive, powerful hope for the future—both personally and organizationally. She builds trust in others, and keeps the heart included in all processes. These leaders develop a personal repertoire of inspirational stories, connect personally with others, and value them individually and corporately. They walk a daily path, with an even attitude, consistent energy and influential passion and encouragement. They are aware that everything they do, from the quickest e-mail to the grand company annual meeting, will have influence. They are intentional about their influence.

Influencing Inspiration and Leadership requires a strong sense of vision and values (personal and organizational), an understanding of personal passions and the desire to encourage and inspire others, and influence in a positive way. This Legacy Practice looks at challenges as opportunities for growth and innovative potential, and places more importance on the development and well-being of others, rather than self. That's a tall order, and one that can only come from an honest review of personal heart health. Not the organ, but the attitude. If your heart resonates with this Legacy Practice, you already have the makings for a Legacy Leader. We have said that this practice is the heart of Legacy Leadership, and these competencies and skills are the heart of a Legacy Leader.

Reflection

1. How are you effectively applying, and living, Legacy Practice 3: Influencing Inspiration and Leadership for leadership legacy?

2. Can you say that you "understand" your team members as individuals— that is, do you KNOW them, know their abilities, know their challenges and show your understanding? How does understanding your team members help you become more of an influencer?

3. What specific areas would you like to develop pertaining to this Legacy Practice?

Next Steps

3

If you want to inspire others, you must first be inspired yourself. The Development Guide is a good place to begin becoming a legacy influencer.

a) The **10 Critical Success Skills:** Core competencies for Legacy Practice 3
b) **Consideration:** Professional Development *(Questions to guide your development as an Influencer of Inspiration and Leadership)*
c) **Essence:** Being a Legacy Leader *(The BE-Attitudes of the Influencer of Inspiration and Leadership)*
d) **Application:** Putting it to Work *(Steps for applying Legacy Practice 3)*
e) **Legacy Shifts:** Expected Outcomes
    (Shifts in behavior and environment that can be expected as a result of applying this Legacy Practice)

The Development Guide for Legacy Practice 3 begins on page 233. Learn how you can intentionally influence and inspire others.

Chapter
FOUR

Legacy Practice 4

	1 **Holder of Vision and Values**™	
2 **Creator of Collaboration and Innovation**™	3 **Influencer of Inspiration and Leadership**™	**4 Advocator of Differences and Community**™
	5 **Calibrator of Responsibility and Accountability**™	

Even the smallest of particles
in our universe does not exist in isolation.
It is part of an entire galaxy
or community of particles.
Each is unique,
bringing different qualities to the whole.

Most often, however,
the whole is what makes the impact,
what makes us stand
in advocacy, applause, and often awe.
Yet without the particles,
the whole ceases to exist.

FOUR: Legacy Practice 4

MAKING A WHOLE FROM ALL THE PARTS
Advocating Differences and Community

4

The fog and early chill of a fall evening settled around the fans gathered in the stands to cheer their local school team. A steady drone of voices could be heard as they waited for the teams in a cross-town rivalry to take the field.

Suddenly cheers erupted, and everyone was on their feet as the game finally began. In the sea of faces seen in the stands, one is very familiar. He is the one shouting words of encouragement, singling out each player by name and personalizing his support with a voice that carries over all the others. His enthusiasm for his team is visible, and very audible. Parents and students turn and smile knowingly at him. Who is he? The ever-present, ever-championing school principal, who has taken to the stands, and taken a stand, for his players, his school, his community.

Earlier that day he sat in his office assuring the janitor that problems with his impending retirement would be straightened out soon—he guaranteed it. He was seen in the hallway encouraging a teacher to take some new continuing education courses that would be just right for the classes she would be teaching next year. He frowned at a piece of gutter missing on the gymnasium and jotted a quick note to see that it was fixed soon, mentally rehearsing his explanation of student test scores tomorrow at the district office. As he passed the gym he stopped to watch a young teacher struggle to coach a particularly sassy group of teens who seemed to know more about the sport than the coach. He smiled in remembrance of his own early days of coaching. He would make some time to talk with this coach and share some tips, maybe even suggest a different sport. As he settled back at his desk, he finalized the arrangements for a new faculty member. He had been thinking for some time that the school really needed another science teacher, one particularly suited to deal with certain subjects, one who would bring in a fresh approach, a different strength to this already diverse and strong team of teachers. He looked forward to welcoming this new addition to his staff next fall. And as the bell rang for the first class of the day, he was just beginning a conversation with a student who needed guidance in choosing a college suited to her strengths. The final bell of the day would find him in the student parking lot, sitting in the front seat of the souped-up car of another senior struggling with whether to continue school or enter the military after graduation.

> He is the ultimate advocate — for one, and for all.

The life of a school principal or head master is a busy one. He or she is responsible for the overall operation of the school, including finances, building maintenance, personnel and staff, public relations, school policies, discipline, coordination of the instructional program and curriculum, excellence of student learning, and staff development, just to name a few. As daily tasks are accomplished, however, there is a driving force that shapes his or her actions. This school principal has become the champion and advocate for not only his school, but each and every student and staff member, parent and community interest. He actively seeks a well-rounded faculty and carefully assigns their positions to yield the greatest learning in students. He is emotionally connected to each student, desiring their success and future achievement, and doing what he can to advocate for each, whenever and wherever. He works tirelessly to cement all the players together into one community, exalting their combined differences that make them strong and effective, meeting the expectations of parents, district and community. He will shout from the bleachers until he has lost his voice, and then he will whisper if he has to. He is the ultimate advocate—for one, and for all.

In many ways, the Legacy Leader is a school principal—we've just exchanged the school hallways for carpeted corporate corridors. Like the principal, he is often tasked with too much, but he knows that those tasks all contribute to the advocacy of his team, his department, his organization and his community. The tasks are necessary to meet the passion that every Legacy Leader has for individuals, for differences, for strengths and for community success. And the passion drives the tasks.

> A leader cannot **do** this, if he or she cannot **be** it.

An advocate is one who stands firm in support. It is about *being* someone who is courageous enough to take a stand, and stay standing. It means having a well-defined sense of right, and the internal strength to defend it. A leader cannot *do* this, if he or she cannot *be* it. It is an unfortunate truth in business today that we do not find too many people who are so clear about who they are that they are willing to take a firm stand regardless of consequences. A Legacy Leader is a ready advocate for what is right, which often involves risk. The word advocator was selected for this practice because it carries more strength than defender or sponsor. This is about internal commitment to causes, practices and people. Legacy Practice 4 is about that kind of strength in promoting differences for the good of the community.

Differences distinguish people or things from other people or things. Varied experiences, perspectives, backgrounds, styles and personalities in an environment that promotes relationships can be one of the richest means of organizational health.

> It is important to understand that "differences," in this Legacy Practice, go well beyond cultural, personal and ethnic "diversity."

It is important to understand that "differences," in this Legacy Practice, go well beyond cultural, personal and ethnic "diversity." These differences are not necessarily about external appearance, gender, age, orientation or faith. Every person has a unique style, a different perspective, diverse experiences. We are all "wired" differently. Advocating differences is actively being inclusive of all these varied "uniquenesses" in individuals. An advocator of differences intentionally promotes differences and values them for the organizational whole, acknowledges his or her personal set of biases, stereotypes and labels, then seeks to overcome them. This Legacy Leader knows how he or she is different, that we are all different, and seeks to discover how others see the world and individual situations. Great leaders are actually curious about differences, truly desire to learn more about them, and purposely reframe how they think and how they approach people who are "different" from themselves.

Community is a group of people with shared interests working together to achieve shared success. The community advocate is always looking for the strengths of individuals to add to the success of the whole, and sees beyond the boundaries of individuals, teams or departments. These leaders are knowledgeable about the perspectives, strengths, needs and offerings available from all sources, and actively seek to lift up others, including those "outside" immediate corporate or departmental lines. They have identified their own strengths, and help others to discover and value their strengths and potential contributions. They are always aware of and consistently promote the added benefits of inclusion.

The Legacy Leader will advocate differences and community by seeking relationships with team members, by discovering, acknowledging, and accepting differences in those relationships, and by promoting individual strengths and perspectives for the greater whole of the organization. This leader will promote and combine differences into a unified whole, and then stand in support of this community as it builds relationships—both inside and outside the organization—that enlarge and expand the growth of the community and the success of the organization.

On July 4, 1776, the Journals of the Continental Congress recorded, *"Resolved, That Dr. Franklin, Mr. J. Adams and Mr. Jefferson, be a committee, to bring in a device for a seal for the United States of America."* A "great seal" was needed to represent this fledgling new country. Congress chose three distinguished members of the committee that drafted the Declaration of Independence to develop such a seal. These men were no doubt some of the brightest among the leaders of the new nation. However, their conceptual artistry left much to be desired. They even consulted a respected artist, Pierre Eugène Du Simitière, but their combined efforts to capture the ideology of the United States in a seal left Congress flat. Their suggestions were tabled. While it took several more years and quite a few more attempts to create a visual seal that Congress could approve in 1782, there was one thing everyone agreed on from the start—the motto. Du Simitière's drawing didn't make it, but the words he printed at the bottom did: *E pluribus unum.* This Latin phrase well represented the new country's ideals. It literally means "From many, (comes) one." That is the spirit of Legacy Practice 4, with a twist. Our motto could be *"From many strengths comes united success."* We won't even attempt the Latin equivalent.

Advocating: Taking a Stand

You may not have to *sit* in the stands, but you will have to *take a stand*—perhaps many stands, over the course of your leadership. "Taking

> Without the ability to take a stand, leadership fails and crumbles at the first sign of trouble.

a stand" is defined as adopting a position, adhering to a certain policy or attitude, and upholding, supporting and defending something or someone. In short, the person taking a stand becomes an advocate for a person, practice or cause. Without the ability to take a stand, leadership fails and crumbles at the first sign of trouble. Just as important, however, is the ability to know what to advocate, and when not to take a stand. Abraham Lincoln, in his usual simple but profound manner, said the following: *"Stand with anybody that stands right, stand with him while he is right and part with him when he goes wrong."* Good advice for anyone, especially the leader. There are three basic components to being an advocate that can be derived from President Lincoln's simple statement:

1. Always stand for right
2. Always stand with those who stand for right
3. Do not stand for what is not right

Taking a stand in business applications involves standing firm for certain policies, procedures, vision, or practices that you as leader think are right. The Legacy Leader first *knows* what is right, before *doing* what is right. He or she is completely on top of all business situations to know when a person, practice or cause is right for the organization, for the strategic vision or plan, and whether it is right ethically and morally—and personally. If you know it is right, you also need to know how you will take a stand for it—how you will advocate it—especially if it is threatened in any way. A Legacy Leader makes a commitment to stand also with *people* who are right, whether advocating for the person, a cause, practice or action of the person. The leader may sometimes even have to advocate *self*, rather than someone else. Both positions are common in business, and the ability to take, and hold, these stands is necessary for effective leadership.

And, perhaps just as important, a great leader knows when to *not* stand with or for a person, practice or cause that is *not* right. You need the wisdom and discernment to know the difference, and your leadership stand reveals your understanding, wisdom and integrity. If we are pulled over for a traffic violation, and exclaim our innocence because we had no idea there was such a law, a police officer will patiently explain "ignorance of the law is no excuse." Ignorance of the facts before you take a stand, or not take a stand, is no excuse either.

The Greeks had a word for this kind of advocating leader which provides us a deeper understanding of this practice. It is the word "parakletos" which literally means *one who has been called upon to help.* The

Greeks used this word to indicate a legal advisor, a pleader, or advocate, who comes forward on behalf of and as the representative of another. The greater meaning, however, is found in the root of this word, "parakaleo." It is an action verb which means to "come alongside" to provide aid, comfort, or share a burden. A Legacy Leader is not just an advocate, but one who comes alongside another. Does this describe you?

You may have heard the expression, *"the person who stands for nothing will fall for anything."* This is true in every area of life, even in business. Great leaders stand for something, and make commitments to lead by certain values, beliefs and actions. And if this leader makes these values public, he or she is asking for increased accountability and risks the scrutiny and criticism of others. Even without public expression, the manner in which you work reveals what you value, and what you stand for. Will it hold up under pressure?

Mentoring:
Advocating Individuals _____

Constantly and carefully raising the visibility of those you lead, making a commitment to their leadership development, is one of the best ways to promote the success of the entire organization. As an advocate for individuals, you are a sponsor, supporter, guide and champion, taking a stand for each individual's success—in other words, a mentor. And when individuals succeed, organizations succeed.

Mentoring is popular in today's leadership circles. Most of the time the word elicits visions of formal organizational programs, training and structured systems for mentoring. These programs are very important for many reasons, and the case for mentoring is compelling for the obvious purposes of employee development, productivity and engagement. Yes, everyone knows mentoring programs are powerful tools within organizations. For this Legacy Practice, however, mentoring applies not to just a program, but to an attitude. Whether or not an officially sanctioned mentoring program exists within the organization, a leader's attitude is always that of a mentor, seeking opportunities to develop others and raise their visibility. This attitude is others-centered, not self-centered, and sincerely desires to build leaders and encourage growth in those around you.

A national service company is known for its mentoring program where potential managers are identified, coached and positioned on taskforces nationwide to increase their visibility and give them opportunities to receive extra leadership and managerial training. These high-potential employees are often moved around to various positions and processes within the

> Mentoring is first an attitude, and a fiercely held value, that great leaders develop other great leaders.

company in order to display their skills, affinities, passions and strengths and become well-rounded and multi-talented assets. Not only does this practice benefit the employees who are showcased, it also benefits the company which develops a rich talent pool for internal hires. Employee retention is dramatically increased, cutting the financial drain to hire and train new employees. There are many advantages to an organizational mentoring program, but you don't have to wait for one to practice mentoring and developing others. Mentoring is first an attitude, and a fiercely held value, that great leaders develop other great leaders.

Spend some time considering your mentoring skills and attitudes with your current team members. It is a worthwhile activity to take a sheet of paper and build a table like the one below. It can provide you a simple but solid plan for mentoring others.

Team member you are, or could be, mentoring now	For what purpose, or reason(s)?	What do/can you do, to mentor this person? *(specific actions)*	What development opportunities do/can you provide?	How do/can you raise this person's visibility?
1.				
2.				
3.				
4.				
5.				

Also consider the consequences of *not* mentoring the people you have listed in your table. Mentoring can make the difference between retention and loss of employees. We all need mentors, and if we don't find them in one place, we generally seek them somewhere else. Mentoring and development don't require formal programs, although they can be helpful to provide structure. Mentoring *does* require the attitude and heart desire to grow others.

Strength in Differences

Thankfully, we are not all the same. Each of us has different strengths. There are differences in our strengths and strength in our differences. A Legacy Leader advocates for a strengths-based culture, where everyone works from their strengths. Such a culture is built any number of ways, but the essence is to identify the strengths of your workers and align them with the needed outcomes for your area of responsibility. The focus is always on strengths. We all know it is good business to have the right fit for employees and desired outcomes. There are many excellent programs available to guide you through the steps of doing this. That is not our purpose here.

> Individual strengths are measured and matched to expected and desired organizational results.

The focus of this competency is to be sure that you are actively *advocating*, promoting and encouraging, building and preserving this culture. This needs to be an intentionally and consistently *held* value for you and your organization. It involves first *knowing* the strengths of your individual team members, and then placing them in the right position to showcase those strengths to contribute to overall organizational success. Individual strengths are measured and matched to expected and desired organizational results. This exercise is not a one-time event. It is an ongoing diligence that allows you to become highly "in tune" with your team members, knowing their strengths and continuing to assign work or place them into positions where those strengths shine and they achieve the desired outcomes. As positions or tasks change, this dynamic is altered, requiring consistent monitoring and appropriate recalibration. Employees consistently working from their strengths happens by intentional design, requiring effort, intelligent direction and skillful execution.

Like any good idea, the concept of a strengths-based culture can also be taken to the extreme, out of balance. Be careful of the directives of some to disregard weaknesses and pour all your efforts into developing strengths. Avoid the temptation to cover up unacceptable or weak performance *(your own, or that of others)* with attention only to strengths. While it is true that at times efforts to upgrade weaknesses in individuals is a futile and frustrating effort, attention to strengths only is never a cover for tolerance of unacceptable performance, which may or may not be due to a person's "weaknesses." Try to avoid using this, or allowing others to use it, as a "cop-out" for excellence.

We have stated that this Legacy Practice expands the commonly understood concept of *diversity*. Yes, we advocate for diversity in the workplace, and all that those words imply regarding cultural, ethnic and personal differences. Having optimally functioning and producing teams of individuals in business, however, means insisting on diversity at many levels. These are just some of the diversities and differences that contribute to high-functioning teams:

- ☐ Cultural and ethnic backgrounds
- ☐ Skills and competencies
- ☐ Experiences
- ☐ Education
- ☐ Perspectives
- ☐ Personality
- ☐ Styles
- ☐ Ways of learning, thinking and processing

There are many other kinds of diversity valued in a team environment. You can add to this list those appropriate for your area. As you develop your teams, it is important to remember that your goal is not to build a colony of clones. Replicating only your strengths—and your weaknesses—won't build a diverse community. And it won't get you the needed perspectives, abilities, judgments and wisdom that can combine for a powerfully productive team. You need to stretch a little, trust a lot, and exhibit humility when advocating differences for a stronger community.

Organizations may make deliberate, planned attempts at hiring individuals with "diversity," giving their HR departments guidelines and "quotas." That is only a first step. These diverse people are then shaped into collaborative teams which value, respect and draw collective community strength from this diversity. This is where many organizations fail—not at *being* diverse, but in *working together* in that diversity. For some reason, diversity is a subject that many like to sweep under the corporate carpet. Instead, we can be exploring and exalting diversity, and putting it to work. Great leaders have the courage to reveal differences, even promote them. They will capitalize on their personal strengths, admit their weaknesses, then surround themselves with others who offer unique strengths to fill in the gaps. It's time to actually *point out* differences, discuss uniquenesses, then work together to build them into a strong collaborative community.

> Great leaders have the courage to reveal differences, even promote them.

A Connoisseur of Talent

We most often think of a connoisseur as someone qualified or competent to judge the arts, fine food, or rare antiques—one who has cultivated a "sense of the best." This sense is not limited to fine arts and food. Business can have

a bounty of such discerning judges as well. If you are actively mentoring
and advocating for the success of the individuals you lead, you will have
opportunity to *sample* the abundance of their talents. A *Connoisseur of
Talent* is one who is able to recognize and value ability, then actively use
that ability as a resource for goal achievement.
Ability itself may at times be in limited supply,
but the ability to *recognize* ability is often even
more scarce. If you are advocating differences
and diversity in talents and strengths, you do it
by becoming a connoisseur of talent. A Legacy
Leader has a cultivated sense of the best in talent
and diverse strengths. A connoisseur becomes a connoisseur by practice,
not by accident. Careful and deliberate observation, combined with
developed discernment and testing, earns the connoisseur this title, and the
organization greater rewards.

> ...an unceasing
> cultivation
> of a sense
> of the best.

Athletic coaches in today's professional sports are accomplished
connoisseurs of talent. When teams draft potential players, these players
have obviously demonstrated some talent and strengths at specific positions
and are generally labeled and marketed by their position of experience.
However, if the football coach sees the second string quarterback or tight
end showing potential for being a star wide receiver, the wise coach will
allow this player opportunity to build this skill and may even shake the
team up a bit by moving him into this position. In every sport, coaches
learn quickly to develop this ability to recognize ability. It is an unceasing
cultivation of a sense of the best. The difference between going home to
clean out lockers before the playoffs or continuing on to win the Super Bowl
depends on recognizing the best and making the best use of it for ultimate
community success.

Throw Open
the Borders _____

Recognizing strengths, becoming a connoisseur of talent and advocating a strengths-based culture is not limited to functional, team or departmental boundaries. To make the most of any organization's greatest resource—its people—these invisible lines of demarcation need to be crossed. There are a lot of companies chasing a limited talent pool in business. It is somewhat frenetic out there, as business scrambles to grab up the best and brightest. Skilled and knowledgeable people are hard to find—and retain. However, these rich resources can often be mined, and cultivated and polished, from existing internal people sources. They just might be right under your nose. Legacy Leaders look for cross-functional opportunities where unique talent might be developed.

The variety of differences to be promoted within an organization and within a team can extend across functions, across teams and across departments—even across seniority levels, if appropriate. If you want your organization to function better, as well as it can, you are willing to be realistic, practical and smart about who does what, regardless of common "taboos." A great leader is one willing to take risks to develop talent by stepping over lines and throwing open the borders.

If Susan has proven herself to be a good organizer, why is John doing that job? If John has exhibited observable negotiating skills, why is he still organizing while Alex is struggling in negotiation functions? Some of this is just good, old-fashioned common sense (a scarcity in itself these days, and not so common). Some of this is having the fortitude to cross previously "untouchable" and traditionally hands-off boundaries. It takes courage to buck the "that's-the-way-we've-always-done-it" syndrome by advocating development of your people across traditional lines. If you ignored function, team and departmental boundaries, and even ignored seniority, have you ever considered how you would re-assign these people? Think seriously about who would be doing what and why. Now, consider also any valid reasons why you *can't* do this. (There may be some.)

Stepping over boundaries involves observation, recognition, common sense (logic) and risk. It is smarter to apply logic to the work process by seeking cross-functional opportunities (and other boundaries to cross) to develop talent and work more efficiently. Real results often rest in logic, not politics and arbitrary borders.

> **If groups or teams or even individuals work as "silos," confusion, chaos and tumbling profits can reign.**

Crossing boundaries is also about bringing down walls that separate groups into silos rather than uniting as a whole community. An organization is a whole made up of many parts. These parts will take the form of departments, teams, project groups, leadership levels and many other area or function designations. In order for the whole to function properly, each part collaborates wholly with the others. If they do not, the old adage "the left hand doesn't know what the right hand is doing" defines, and then diminishes, business processes. If this is true, if groups or teams or even individuals work as "silos" (unattached and independent), confusion, chaos and tumbling profits can reign.

A Legacy Leader seeks opportunity for cross-department or inter-department collaboration, lines of communication, and information and talent sharing conduits. It is said that opportunity knocks on a door, but inter-departmental collaboration requires a bridge. A door can be shut.

Build a bridge instead, allowing free access between departments, areas or teams. This bridge is built on trust, and is made strong by the resulting diversity it promotes. The parts make a whole community when the bridge of collaboration spans the gaps between parts. It is, of course, much easier to be a silo than build a bridge. Building and maintaining bridges between departments, peers or other organizational groups or individuals is hard work, time consuming and challenging—but well worth the effort. In fact, as the face of business continues to change, it will be mandatory.

Epic failures in business and government can almost always be linked to a lack of inter-department collaboration that breeds silo operations. Almost every time our world suffers a natural or man-made disaster, local government responses are found to be woefully lacking in collaborative efforts, which contributes to the greater tragedy and magnitude of the disaster. Crossing department or function boundaries doesn't seem to come naturally to us. We tend to prefer to hole up in our own comfort zones, thinking all is well, and ignoring the greater world (and departments) around us. This "comfortable" behavior is dangerous, both for individuals and for entire organizations. Individuals functioning as silos often think they have all the answers. As the saying goes, these people most likely didn't understand the questions. Work groups, teams, departments and other organizational clusters or collectives quite often work as busy little bees in their

> Draw up the blueprints for new bridges that will advocate differences and add diversity to strengthen the whole organization.

designated hives, loyal to and aware only of their work, their function or their role—their hive. It is easy to slip into the "self-contained" have-all-the-answers mode. *No one*, no department has all the answers.

Take a look at the collaborative bridges that exist between departments in your area of responsibility right now, and determine which still need building. Consider how the existing bridges were built, how they are maintained, and how new ones can be constructed. Thoughtfully define the benefits to the organization as a whole, and to your area as a part, gained as a result of this collaboration. Draw up the blueprints for new bridges that will advocate differences and add diversity to strengthen the whole organization.

Contemplate
the Ripples

Organizational boundaries delineate many smaller communities or entities within a company, including departments, teams, management and leadership levels—even individuals. Crossing these boundaries for talent development and collaboration is a Legacy Practice, but still keeps us thinking inside the organizational box. These borders define *intra*-organizational boundaries. Yet there are greater borders than these, and a Legacy Leader considers the impact of actions on the greater community, the one beyond organizational boundaries. What exactly is this "greater community?" *Extra*-organizational boundaries include vendors, subcontractors, other service providers, local community groups or concerns. And one group that is quite often lost in the shuffle—the customer. To comprehend the scope of the greater community, unfold those unwieldy organizational charts and then start tracing and tracking outward, beyond the company. Exactly who and what does your organization touch now—and will in the future?

A development company purchased an historic building in a well-established section of town.

The leaders of this company quickly found themselves embroiled in community fear and anxiety. Maria led the team handling this new acquisition. Her company had originally planned to level the old dilapidated building, and replace it with a modern office complex, their goal being to revitalize the area. But now they were dealing with the extreme trepidation from tenants and community leaders about demolition of their beloved historic building. As Maria worked diligently with the community, she began to see that there could be an even greater opportunity. She put together a development plan that allowed for restoration rather than replacement, with almost the same number of square feet of tenant space. When she presented the plan to the group, she relayed the distinct advantages of branding in the area by keeping residents and community leaders happy while maintaining the goal of revitalization. Maria's plan was approved, and as the renovation got underway, she held regular town hall progress meetings, keeping the community advised and seeking input, as an important part of project communications. The resulting building project was a huge success which actually generated more welcomed media attention than they could have ever hoped for otherwise. Keeping the greater community informed and involved resulted in a far better project and return on investment for this company.

> Whether speaking of the environment, the hip bones connected to the thigh bones, separation degrees, or small and large organizations, it is an inescapable truth that everything is in some way connected.

It is not unusual for people to become paralyzed, on occasion, with the fear of making a mistake. Carefully considering the greater community impact is perhaps one of the best ways to eliminate, or at least greatly reduce, that fear. When the impact of the actions of an organization, or individual leader, is thoughtfully evaluated in advance, tracking them within and as far out beyond the organization as possible, the chance that these actions will be mistakes is greatly reduced. Whether speaking of the environment, the hip bones connected to the thigh bones, separation degrees, or small and large organizations, it is an inescapable truth that everything is in some way connected. And much as we might think or act otherwise, what we do affects other people and other systems.

Here's a good exercise to give you a picture of your greater community. It might seem a bit elementary to begin with, but take the time to do it anyway. Making a simple drawing to illustrate the impact you have on your greater community can dramatically change how you lead, and how you live. Draw a little box in the center of a large piece of paper and label it with you and your area of responsibility. Around this center box draw more boxes to indicate all the other departments, areas, teams, etc. within your organization. Draw lines to show your inter-dependency. Add any other entities or communities that show inter-department impacts. Draw a large circle around all of these boxes—what is inside represents the organization. Now draw more boxes on the outside of the big circle. These represent all those groups and individuals that your organization touches. Label them, and show who they touch, and so on. It is a striking way to get a feel for who and what needs to be considered when you and your organization are about to take certain actions. If you continue this exercise to show the "ripple" effects of other people and groups on one another, coming from you (the center), it is also an eye-opening representation of your legacy as a leader. Are you getting the picture? Save your drawing and refer to it as you consider the impact of your actions on the greater community.

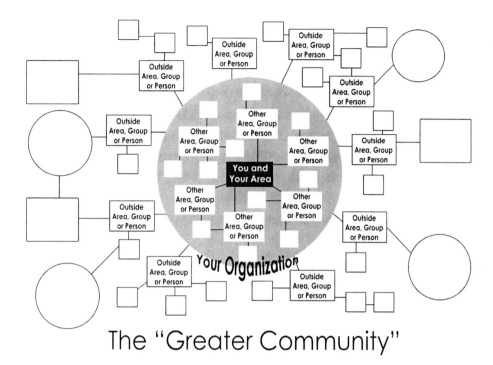

The "Greater Community"

Rotary Club International® adopted a motto in 1943 for its members, to guide their personal and professional lives. It is just as powerful and true today as it was then. It is called the *Four-Way Test*: Of the things we think, say or do:

1) Is it the TRUTH?
2) Is it FAIR to all concerned?
3) Will it build GOODWILL and BETTER FRIENDSHIPS?
4) Will it be BENEFICIAL to all concerned?

This motto is a great reminder of the need to consider the impact of our actions on others. Think about what other questions could be asked, and are particularly appropriate and relevant for your area of responsibility.

Remember that as you regard the ripple effect on the greater community, you are doing so as an advocate of the whole. As a Legacy Leader, it is your job to be sure everyone wins, whenever possible, or to minimize or eliminate (if possible) any negative impacts. Many people try to skip or ignore this process, since it may be time consuming. But in the end, the rewards of community wellness and strength far outweigh the time investment. The benefits and payoff are often beyond your ability to foresee.

Stay Connected, Keep Talking

If you are to advocate for the whole, in order to best assess the impact of actions, leaders need to also have some established dialogue and involvement with these internal and external groups—so that potential impacts can be fully known. This will require you to stay connected to all communities, inside and out, maintaining open dialogue and involvement. If you have not taken the time yet to draw out and identify your internal and external "communities," we recommend you stop right here and do it now. If leaders are going to consider the impact of their actions on the greater community, beyond organizational boundaries, quite obviously they are first able to *identify* that larger community, and determine how to maintain open channels.

The organization, as a whole, is part of an even greater whole. When all parts share information and involve one another, knowledge is transferred more quickly and efficiently, and the whole machine runs smoother, moving in the same direction. Dialogue and consistent communication is essential to community partnerships. Obviously, a great leader possesses great communication skills. But unless he or she understands the importance of shared mutual interest, interlocking community contributions, common bonds and goals and the even greater importance of consistent communication and maintenance of regular dialogue, these internal and external communities will not stay healthy. This is true for relationships and partnerships inside or outside the organization.

> What is communicated, how it is communicated, and when, are far more important than merely a dialogue for the sake of dialogue.

Beware the old trap, however, that more is always better. The quantity of communication does not necessarily have any bearing on its quality. We tend to think that good communication is a lot of communication. We bury each other in flooded e-mail inboxes, wipe out entire forests to send needless memos and fill the airwaves with chatter, thinking all along that we can certainly pat ourselves on the back for being such grand communicators. Meaningful dialogue can be lost amidst the cacophony of chatter. What is communicated, how it is communicated, and when, are far more important than merely a dialogue for the sake of dialogue. That is "token talk" and doesn't serve any purpose. Communication between internal and external communities is well planned, carefully constructed, and diligently maintained for quality and results.

In this age of global alliances, liaisons and partnerships, it is even more imperative that the maintenance of meaningful dialogue is held as a top priority. Like many other companies, a large top-brand manufacturing company with a long history of successful business in America has "gone global." With a gung-ho attitude and huge financial investment to establish plants and markets in countries across the globe, one missing element was soon evident—interaction, involvement and conversation at individual local levels where these markets were being developed. This company discovered early on that the American way of business cannot be plunked down in a foreign land and culture and be expected to flourish with a one-size-fits-all philosophy. In one particular market a long-awaited and publicly proclaimed acquisition was terminated because all the parties had different

Successful strategies depend on whole systems thinking.

expectations, and different means of achieving them—a result of different ways of doing business. As is usually the case, the harder lessons are generally the best lessons. This company has since given great attention to achieving a policy of conscious interaction with local communities, developing relationships, learning cultures and ways of doing business, and then bringing back that knowledge inside the corporation to share with internal constituents, before leaping into risky ventures.

As you learn to see your organization as many parts to a whole, systems working within a greater system, chances are these systems are much wider and broader than you have been thinking. Successful strategies depend on whole systems thinking, beyond the cubicles, hallways and corridors you can see from your office. Get a grip on the big picture. Look for any disconnects, or gaps in partnership. Tie up any drifting boats that need to be anchored with the fleet and run periodic diagnostics on all your internal and external communities to be sure you are connected and involved. Check to see that your communication serves to enlighten, not encumber, and determine if your perhaps once well-oiled machine might need a tune-up.

Creating an Inclusive Environment

It's time now to bring all these differences, diversity, greater communities and partners together by creating and promoting an inclusive environment that unites all the parts into a whole with a common focus. This is the final important element of advocating for differences and community. We could summarize this chapter by stating it as a formula:

$$\frac{\text{Differences/diversity + collaborative community}}{X}$$
$$\text{advocating for an inclusive united environment}$$
$$=$$
$$\underline{\text{common focus}} \rightarrow \text{SUCCESS}$$

Combine healthy differences to make broad diversity, add a collaborative, communicating community and multiply the whole thing by an inclusive united environment, mix it up with a strong advocate, and you get common focus, which encourages success. Simple formula—and it works—but only if all the elements are in place. Promoting differences and diversity only creates islands adrift in the community sea if the inclusive and united environment is missing.

Building an inclusive culture that is magnetized and energized into common focus begins by systematically identifying each component—every

> You will find opportunities around every cubicle—if you're looking for them.

person, every team, every division—and actively ensuring that each knows and understands its role and function in the greater whole, and that it is not there for individual recognition, but as a *contribution* to the whole. This is the cornerstone of bringing everyone together as a single community united with a common cause, but there are many practical actions that can be taken to promote an inclusive environment. You will find opportunities around every cubicle for this—if you're looking for them.

Before action steps can be taken, however, something much more difficult, and more foundational, needs to be in place—*the right attitude. Your attitude.* It begins with you. Your attitude dictates your words and actions and impacts everyone around you. *"It's not about me"* is the attitude of a Legacy Leader. Can you imagine what your company could accomplish if everyone had this attitude? Sit back and watch the fences fall, the silos crumble and the bottom line soar. Unfortunately, this attitude is often very rare in the corporate venue—anywhere for that matter. It all starts with one. Are you the one? Once a leader adopts this attitude—humbly, honestly and not arrogantly acting a part—the rest of the steps toward an inclusive environment will be obvious. This leader will be alert to possibilities that bridge gaps, include all differences and parts, and generate a community-wide common focus.

Honestly rate your attitude on the "It's Not About Me Scale" and consider why you gave yourself this rating and what you are prepared to do to become a "perfect 10."

Where Do You Score on the "It's Not About Me Scale?"

1	2	3	4	5	6	7	8	9	10
It's ALL about me							It's NOT about me		

Neither independence nor dependence will promote an inclusive environment. Independent people don't need or want the influence of others. They prefer to do it all themselves, and take all the glory. Dependent people rely on others to get what they want, and become exhausting rather than stimulating. An attitude and culture of inter-dependence, honest and community sharing of efforts, resources and focus, drive the greatest successes.

The Bottom Line

Advocating Differences and Community allows individuals and teams to discover strengths in both commonality and diversity that can be instrumental in the growth of the individual, the community and the organization. These leaders model an attitude of connectedness and inclusion, don't need to get the "credit" for successes and have no hidden agendas other than advancing and celebrating community achievement. They encourage, promote and protect such advocacy and draw together individuals who contribute diverse perspectives for a greater good, and who will model the endorsement and leveraging of differences into added value for the whole. These Legacy Leaders will defend, support and speak up for individuals, differences, and community. The *advocating* leader is sure of who he or she is, and therefore comfortable to step outside of personal ego to spotlight others, and wholly embraces the concept of "E pluribus unum."

Being an advocate often means working against natural human tendency. It is not instinctual behavior. Before any leader can be a true *Legacy* Leader, he or she embraces a position of being others-centered rather than self-centered. This means we make a hard choice that defies natural behavior for this species, a choice that exalts the richness (and rewards) of community rather than the empty advancement of self only. Advocating Differences and Community means building a relational environment where trust, respect and discovery thrive. In this environment diverse perspectives open new doors and build new bridges to opportunity and possibility. There is no "turf protection," comfort zones, snap judgments or labels and prejudices. There is only inclusive expectation for what can be achieved together.

Reflection

1. How are you effectively applying, and living, Legacy Practice 4: Advocating Differences and Community for leadership legacy?

2. Can you, at any given time, easily state the strengths of each of your team members, and say with assurance, that each one is in the right place, doing the right thing, working from their strengths?

3. What specific areas would you like to develop pertaining to this Legacy Practice?

Next Steps

Do you want to know how to model connectedness, inclusion and promote both commonality and diversity in order to grow yourself and your organization? Here's what will help you in the Development Guide:

a) The **10 Critical Success Skills:** Core competencies for Legacy Practice 4

b) **Consideration:** Professional Development *(Questions to guide your development as an Advocator of Differences and Community)*

c) **Essence:** Being a Legacy Leader *(The BE-Attitudes of the Advocator of Differences and Community)*

d) **Application:** Putting it to Work *(Steps for applying Legacy Practice 4)*

e) **Legacy Shifts:** Expected Outcomes
(Shifts in behavior and environment that can be expected as a result of applying this Legacy Practice)

The Development Guide for Legacy Practice 4 begins on page 249. Put your learning into practice as you build stronger community.

4

Chapter

FIVE

Legacy Practice 5

1
Holder of Vision and Values™

2	3	4
Creator of Collaboration and Innovation™	**Influencer of Inspiration and Leadership**™	**Advocator of Differences and Community**™

5
Calibrator of Responsibility and Accountability™

There are many English words that end in "ability." The two that perhaps get the least attention are *responsibility* and *accountability*. These are abilities—to respond and then to account for that response. They are the music of the constant dance of progress. Calibration keeps the dance from falling off the stage.

FIVE: Legacy Practice 5

GETTING IT DONE RIGHT
Calibrating Responsibility and Accountability 5

If you were to arrive hours before a concert at Carnegie Hall, or other such grand performance house anywhere in the world, you would most likely see a magnificent instrument taking center stage, glistening black under subdued lighting.

It is large and imposing, casting a long and deep shadow across the polished wood floor. This instrument, unlike others that are often carried on stage, frequently anchors entire symphonies and must be placed before all the others. So for now, it stands alone. Sometimes formally called a *pianoforte* (Italian for "soft-loud"), the piano is an intricately constructed assembly of frame, keys, pedals, wires, bridges, hitch pins and felt hammers, among assorted other parts, pieces and gizmos most of us can't name.

Back at Carnegie Hall, if we came early enough, we might even be so fortunate as to spot a lone figure on stage playing the piano—but not making very beautiful music, at least to our ears. Whether it is an upright, "baby grand," or a full concert-sized Macassar Ebony Steinway & Sons masterpiece, all pianos need one thing—constant tuning. When a piano has been tuned and adjusted by a trained and experienced tuner—an artist, really—the resulting sounds can make grown-ups cry. It is sweet and soothing, lifting spirits beyond physical boundaries. Without tuning, however, a piano is merely a very expensive noisemaker. The critical piece in this musical picture is not necessarily the piano. It is the piano tuner who can enable the piano to do what it was designed to do. Piano tuning is a combination of knowledge, skill, music, mathematics, and artistry—and a love for the powerful *potential* of any piano.

> **Calibrating responsibility and accountability is the most often missed practice of leadership.**

A piano tuner is an accomplished calibrator, which is precisely what the Legacy Leader is. In this Legacy Practice, however, we aren't calibrating pianos—it's a calibration of people and progress to yield a more powerful and successful future. A Legacy Leader will keep checking, keep adjusting, keep tuning until individual and organizational maximum potential are reached and maintained.

Calibrating responsibility and accountability is the most often missed practice of leadership. Leaders can *be* and *do* all the others, and neglect this one—the critical final piece. Everything else depends on it. The words *responsibility* and *accountability* can occasionally cause people to break into a cold sweat and seek immediate cover. We certainly don't want to elicit that kind of response. This curious reaction is due mostly to accountability's frequent association with finger pointing and blame naming. We'll set your minds at ease right now—that is not what this practice is about. Responsibility and accountability are not words to shun, rather words and actions that can take ability into mastery. *This Legacy Practice is all about making the sweet music of success.*

A calibrator "sets the mark," determining the quantitative measurement of success (and desired results). Calibration is done by one who is clear about standards, vision, values, and what is right both personally and organizationally, and measures all behavior against them. This is an automatic, ongoing internal process that never stops. It is a natural, conscious and continual setting of the "mark" and adjusting what is necessary to hit it consistently. It implies a sense of awareness, measurement and appropriate adjustment. Again, it is not just doing, it is being vigilant, accountable, responsible, thoughtful and nimble, with a constant eye on the target. A Legacy Leader is a human thermostat of sorts, always measuring the environment and adjusting as necessary. There is a big difference between a thermo*stat* and a thermo*meter*. When a thermometer measures the environment it is able to monitor only—it can't adjust or regulate that environment. In business a "monitor" merely catches people breaking the rules. Calibrating leaders act like a thermostat, by setting the standard and modeling consistent acceptable behavior, naming it, and adjusting it as necessary. In this illustration the temperatures measured are the desired results.

Responsibility is the ability to respond correctly to—and meet—stated expectations. It is the ownership of what you have been tasked to do. Calibrators of Responsibility have very clearly defined vision and values, for themselves and their organization, know instinctively what is acceptable and "right" behavior, and also know what is not. The leader calibrates the responsible roles within an organization by ensuring that the right people are in the right positions, able to meet stated expectations. In order for others to meet those expectations—*be responsible*—the Legacy Leader provides the tools (content, context, resources) so that a worker can learn and have all that is needed to fulfill their responsibilities and be accountable for process and outcome. The leader is, in other words, ultimately responsible for ensuring that people do those things *for which they are responsible,* and shares responsibility (and challenges) for processes and outcomes that may fall short of desired results to reach the vision. This requires a constant calibration process by which the leader provides a consistent role model of acceptable, expected behavior, ensures measurement of progress toward the vision, and makes no exceptions to the expectations for responsible and acceptable behavior.

> A Calibrator of Accountability respects others, realizes that accountabilities are shared, and provides a consistent role model of *personal* accountability.

Accountability is the obligation to explain or justify conduct, conditions or circumstances. Accountabilities are those things for which we are responsible, that we can be counted on to accomplish, and expected by others to do. Accountabilities have a part in individual, team, departmental and whole community process. A Calibrator of Accountability respects others, realizes that accountabilities are shared, and provides a consistent role model of *personal* accountability. The leader sets and communicates the expectations, milestones, measurement and requirements of accountabilities. The *great* leader regularly measures accountabilities *and compares* against existing vision and values, making required adjustments. A critical component of this practice is also understanding that the accountability process is a growth process, not an excuse for blame and shame. Legacy Leaders focus on what went right and what can be done differently, instead of what went wrong, holding themselves responsible, and accountable, first. Calibrating accountability means developing plans for making adjustments in standards of behavior as a result of new information or changes, while never compromising vision and values. And this leader also knows how to celebrate and reward the accomplishment of those goals.

As we discussed earlier, the mere mention of the words *responsibility* and *accountability* can create dread, fear and avoidance in the hearts of many. Since the dawn of time, we humans have struggled with these characteristics that serve as a measure of integrity. Regardless of your spiritual or religious experience, most of us have at least heard of the infamous event in the Garden of Eden. We all know the story of Adam and Eve's disobedience and the subsequent fall from grace, introducing sin into a perfect world. What most don't know, however, is the almost humorous exchange between God, and Adam and Eve, as he attempted to hold them accountable for their behavior. When God questioned Adam about his actions, he blamed Eve, and ultimately even blamed God for giving him "the woman." When Eve was asked about her behavior, she blamed the serpent. Neither of them was willing to take responsibility, or be accountable, for their actions. If it weren't so tragic, it would be funny, this conversation standing as a tribute to our natural tendency to blame others rather than be accountable. We choose to be responsible and accountable—we are not incontrovertibly pre-disposed to irresponsibility. Accountability is necessary for growth—in anyone, anywhere. It is a critical part in the development of integrity and the advancement of success.

> A calibrator has the mind of a technician, yet the heart of a passionate artist unlocking potential.

As a balancing point, however, the Legacy Leader realizes that we are all mere mortals and all of us will stumble and even fall from time to time. This also is a normal and expected part of the growth process. Leaders do a high-wire balancing act as they walk the fine line between possible and impossible, reasonable and unreasonable, stretching and breaking, all the while juggling human frailty and potential along the way. To achieve realistic results, and true legacy in this practice, the leader remembers that accountability and responsibility are a partnership that has at its heart the pure best interest of all parties. Accountability can be one of the most powerful tools for dynamic and dramatic growth and results. Consider the piano tuner who knows his practice, yet becomes a master artisan because of his *passion*, not just his skill. He is passionate about the beautiful music the instrument will produce after his tuning. It is as much about attitude as it is aptitude. A calibrator in this Legacy Practice has the mind of a technician, but the heart of a passionate (and compassionate) artist unlocking potential.

The Legacy Leader will calibrate responsibility and accountability by stating and demonstrating standards of behavior, providing clarity about expectations of results, and by ensuring measurement of progress towards vision. He or she will begin this process by defining those things for which all are responsible, including him or herself, and by providing a measurement system and process to evaluate the success of accomplishments and results, and celebrating accomplished goals. These leaders will encourage, promote and protect this calibration value and process by making adjustments for new information and change, providing a consistent role model for personal accountability, standards for behavior and results, and the consistent milestone marking and evaluation of the process toward expected outcomes. And, these leaders will remember that accountability is not a one-way street, and they are likewise responsible and accountable to those they lead.

Legacy Practice 5 is all about execution—getting it done right. When mastered, it is a very positive practice that should elicit excitement, and results—not dread.

We all need to reframe our thinking about responsibility and accountability to delete blame and insert gain. Legacy Practice 5 is all about execution—

getting it done right. When mastered, it is a very positive practice that should elicit excitement, and results—not dread.

Envision, Execute and Evaluate _____

In Legacy Practice 1 we discussed having a well-defined strategic plan for accomplishing the goals of the vision. That practice is about *holding* vision and values, and was designed to help you understand the critical need for a strategic plan, both for the organization as a whole, and for you as a leader in your area of responsibility. After you have envisioned and established your strategy, Legacy Practice 5 is where the "rubber meets the road," so to speak. All other skills, practices and competencies are worthless without this one. It's about *doing* (accomplishing) the vision, and *checking* your progress. Vision is followed by strategy, which is followed by execution, which is followed by measurement—and then adjusted by calibration. All strategy is translated into clearly developed action plans with benchmarks and milestones, and provisions for making adjustments along the way.

Perhaps the best analogy of an action plan is a road map. You have marked your starting point (where you are now) and your final destination (where you want to be). The "benchmarks" and "milestones" are equivalent to the mile markers you pass, indicating you are still on the right road (or not). We have discussed the development of a strategic plan, akin to your overall direction and design to get from point A to point B. Within this master strategic plan *(your map)*, several action plans may be devised along the way to accommodate specific goals *(such as where to have dinner or how to find a hotel with a pool in the heart of Texas in the summer)*. We've also indicated the need to identify and list key performance indicators that serve as your mile markers. The road map is now in place, marked up as a ready navigation tool. The big question is, now that you have begun the journey, how and when do you make course corrections?

Many people spend hours planning, marking up their road maps, then fail to consider actions or policies necessary when strategies and action plans need to change. In this world, not much is fixed or unchanging. What happens when that hotel in Texas has closed, or the road signs for the great restaurant that made you salivate were 30 years old? A world in a constant state of flux is wildly unpredictable, but it is manageable and navigable with thoughtful foresight. Change is anticipated, and plans adapted in real time. Life, and business, are often labyrinthine dances through an ever-changing obstacle course, where flexibility and agility are critical survival skills. A Legacy

Our Journey

STRATEGY: Travel from Point A to Point B by car, pack for hotel but take camping gear, games for kids, plan trip to arrive by Friday.

ACTION PLANS:
- Stop to check maps
- Eat at XYZ Restaurant
- Take scenic route
- Check into Hotel (use campground if no vacancies)
- Meet family at reunion
- Meet friends outside of town
- Check roads for conditions before selecting route
- Take scenic route if time allows
- Visit Historical Monument
- Go fishing from dock with kids
- Watch weather and roads for current conditions

ALTERNATES OR CORRECTIONS:
- Use campground if hotel full
- Ask locals for other good restaurants
- Call ahead for attraction and monument times
- Have picnic in park if attraction not open
- Take R6 to View Point if Scenic Route not open

Leader will have policies (and attitudes) in place to handle change, not just deal with it, but use it as opportunity. Leaders read the road signs and determine whether a wrong turn was made, or when they need to take an alternate route if one road washes out. You want that realization to dawn *before* you are airborne over the cliff.

Planning the journey to a destination is only part of your preparation. Your strategic plan is to not only include every facet of reaching your vision, it also considers policies and planning for executing course corrections. Calibrating responsibility and accountability is at the heart of planning for re-alignment and adjustments to the strategic plan, and subsequent action plans. *Being* a calibrator is foundational to success.

As the journey progresses, the Legacy Leader executes the organization's strategic plan while using appropriate checks and balances to reach the stated and desired goals. "Checks and Balances" is a concept we all know well as a tool to keep government functioning within certain guidelines. It usually refers to a system in which separate entities (like three branches of government) check or monitor the behavior of each other, having the desired effect of keeping an even balance of power. Checks and balances can be applied to an organization as well, not so much to ensure a balance of power, but to provide a method of evaluating and measuring the progress and process of results achievement. A wise leader will detail clearly appropriate checks and balances, both within the organization, and within his or her area of responsibility. Consider how these checks and balances extend beyond departments and functions. Unfold your strategic map to determine if you are successfully executing that plan, on the right road, headed in the right direction. Evaluate your progress through your established checks and balances. Indicate any changes you may have to make to your plan, and how you will refine your doing of this plan.

Keep Your Finger on the Pulse _____

How often do you take your own pulse? Probably not often, unless you are suffering from some medical ailment or monitoring a workout. We assume our hearts are beating normally most of the time. In business, this assumption can be fatal. Like taking a physical pulse, keeping your finger on the pulse of the organization, or the pulse of your area of responsibility, may seem awkward and time consuming. With practice, focus, and commitment, however, this becomes second nature. Without it, you have no measure of the overall health of your area or organization. Individuals,

whole departments and even whole companies can lose sight of first the vision, then the purpose of their existence. When this happens, it is our tendency to get busier or run faster because we sense something is missing but we don't know what. If we don't take the timeouts required

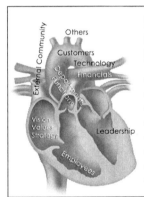

Know Your Organizaztional Pulse

- What's the "pulse?"
- How is it working?
- Is it healthy?
- Does it meet the vision?
- What are the measurements?
- What are the milestones?
- What is the ultimate diagnosis?
- What is the course of "treatment?"

to "check the pulse" we will eventually get worn out, less effective and discouraged. This can happen on every level, from the individual to the corporate community.

The beats of a heart are the milestone status for the health of the body. Every organization has different milestone markers, just like a map has milepost signs. You would not think to travel in an unfamiliar place without consulting a map and the milepost markers on the roads you travel. What are the significant areas, events or points in the organization that serve as your "milestones?" Do you know the status of each one? Glancing at the bottom line alone does not indicate organizational health status. It is only one indicator. Every area is subjected to regular diagnostics. Don't overlook anything—include every aspect and every perspective. Design a program or process to effectively keep your finger on the pulse of every area of your organization, so at any given time, you are aware of your overall organizational health.

Clarity and Commitment

Unless you are a sole proprietor with no employees, you rely on other people to make any progress toward your organizational goals. It is vital that individuals on your team are clear about position responsibilities and how they fit into the organization's direction and deliverables. We all know about job descriptions and the importance of ensuring that team members understand their individual and group responsibilities. The big questions are how, and how often, you give conscious thought to communicating position responsibilities within your functional area and ensuring understanding of mission and organizational fit, as well as deliverable goals.

Making people clear about position responsibilities is not about giving orders. Command and control is arrogant, destroys respect and commitment, and leaves employees with the sense that they are merely worker bees, drones in the hive with only an imposed mandate of mission. If the communication and clarity of position responsibilities is not about giving orders, what *is* it about? What are its components, and what does it look and sound like?

In many organizations today it has become standard policy to hand over an employee manual with all the required regulation rigmarole, legal documents, a written outline of job responsibilities and description, and all the other sundry bits and pieces necessary for employment, ask for a signature of receipt and blissfully believe that we have done our job of new employee indoctrination. Point them in the direction of the desk or cubicle and wish them well. And in many cases, new employees don't even get that much attention or direction. If you were to ask any employer, any leader, what he or she expects of employees, the top answer would be high-performing, creative workers who productively contribute to the organizational bottom line. Then why do we seldom adequately prepare them to be this? And why do we not consider the ongoing attention to maintaining this knowledge and sense of purpose in employees? It goes well beyond the requisite copy of the employee manual and job description.

Knowing their work matters can be the key that unlocks employee creativity, innovation and high performance.

A person's individual responsibilities are woven into the fabric of a team and the larger organization. It is vital to give employees not only a job description and a list of expectations, but also a sense of mission and how they fit into the big picture. Do your employees know their "fit?" Each person needs to be able to have a line of sight from their contributions to the organizational goals and vision. Individuals need to know their value as a single employee, as a member of a team, and as a part of the larger corporate community. A purposely communicated awareness of mission, fit and value leads to a happier and more productive workforce. The knowledge of responsibility is not enough. Knowing their work matters can be the key that unlocks employee creativity, innovation and high performance.

In the movie classic *"It's A Wonderful Life"* Jimmy Stewart's character is given a unique gift—a look at his mission, his purpose and value, and his fit in the lives of others. We're not suggesting that you get sappy or take these concepts to extremes, but it is an irrefutable principle of human dynamics that we all work better and happier when we understand our roles, mission and value to the whole.

Once you have clearly communicated mission and value, organizational "fit," there is yet one additional component absolutely necessary to move forward—commitment. The Legacy Leader will gain commitment from everyone in his or her area of responsibility, and will establish accountabilities with appropriate consequences and rewards. Without followers, there are no leaders. Followers need to have confidence in those they follow, convinced of their integrity and authority. Follower commitment stems from confidence in leadership. Ownership, pride, excellence and passionate production don't usually result when followers are mere order-takers. Generally it is part of our human nature to seek leaders who "deserve" our commitment to follow them. While we may have different values that describe those criteria of commitment, in general it begins with trust, integrity and appropriate authority.

> Marcello's approach to leadership had always been to have everyone understand the priorities, time lines and overlapping responsibilities for results in his division.

When he was hired as the regional director of a biomedical manufacturing company, he quickly realized that this organization's system of performance and accountabilities was sorely lacking. Although goals had been established at the beginning of each year, performance reviews were done only at that time, and current mid-year performance had slipped to average, at best. Employees had difficulty remembering what goals they had set the year before. Marcello knew he had work to do here. He took his management team on a week-long retreat where they collaborated to lay out goals and establish quarterly feedback systems for both production and personal performance levels. As expected, this new approach to performance met with resistance from some, but was gladly embraced by others. He suspected that not everyone would be able to adjust, but he was firmly dedicated to providing the support they needed by keeping goals visible, providing true leadership to reach the goals, and holding himself and everyone accountable. Through coaching and mentoring, and an insistence for—and model of—integrity, Marcello gained commitment from most of

Plan in advance how you will deal with the need for either consequences or rewards.

his team members. Two managers did leave the company because they were either unable or unwilling to commit to this new process, but Marcello rewarded excellence by promoting others from within to fill these positions, strengthening the team. After four quarters of performance reviews, Marcello had gained the full commitment of his management team,

and shifted his entire division into a model of accountability that served as a strong example for other divisions. The bottom line payoff? Greatly increased sales and production, and a loyal, committed workforce.

We can hold people accountable, but unless there are appropriate consequences and rewards, accountability has little meaning. In Marcello's case, he was wise enough to understand this, and chose to reward excellence in tangible, meaningful ways, gaining further commitment. Like everything else in leadership, a good plan for these things can make all the difference in the world. Plan in advance how you will deal with the need for either consequences or rewards. They are *both* necessary for growth.

Although comprehension of the vital need for accountability (and responsibility) may sometimes be elusive, a proper understanding and application of this rarely exercised business essential can actually build greater follower commitment. Employees need to know that they will be held accountable, and also see that this accountability is a beneficial joint venture partnership. The follower is accountable for his or her behavior, and the leader is accountable for *recognition* (as well as personal and professional behavior). *All* behavior is recognized and rewarded, whether that behavior is lacking (negative reward or recognition) or exceptional (positive reward or recognition). *All* behavior has consequences, and contrary to popular use, *consequences* is not a negative word. A consistency in accountability and recognition is critical to building follower confidence. This is another of those natural human dynamics that applies to the business world as well as any other place where humans interact. We have an innate need to know when we've done well, and when we haven't. We do, indeed, get what we reward.

Require the Best, Coach the Rest

We know a Legacy Leader requires peak performance from everyone— including self. However, this simple sounding statement is easier said than done, isn't it? Performance is more than meeting quotas or expectations. Requiring peak performance involves knowing employees and their capabilities, knowing team dynamics and interrelationships, communication, monitoring, accountability and honesty—or truth-telling. People need to know where they stand in order to step forward. Lack of feedback can paralyze momentum. Dishonest feedback can cause costly errors in direction.

Employee feedback needs to be honest, and constructive. Allowing poor performance to go unchecked or unchallenged merely postpones painful realities, and does not give opportunity for improvement. "Letting things slide" is just as bad as turning your area of responsibility into a corporate boot camp. Neither approach works. Honest feedback is at the center, the tipping point, of this teeter-totter. It is like a high-wire walker carrying a balance pole. Dip too far to one side, and you will fall off the wire. Honest constructive feedback allows everyone to keep their balance. Employee coaching and feedback are necessary on a consistent basis, but absolutely imperative when performance does not meet stated expectations.

To provide honest and *successful* feedback and coaching, it is important to fully understand these terms. Feedback in itself is merely information about performance. This can be good or bad. Feedback *with coaching*, however, is what makes the information constructive, useful and dynamic. It is a conversation designed to promote better performance, personal commitment and long-lasting improvement. Coaching is encouragement with accountability for success. It is not sugar-coating, avoidance or denial, or hype. The coaching leader speaks the truth in order to facilitate a positive plan.

Anna was vice president of a large international pharmaceutical company.

The company was growing fast, and so were the complaints. When confronted with these issues, Jelani, the IT manager, could not understand how people could complain when he and his team were doing everything they could just to keep things supplied, repaired and ahead of technology changes. His staff was working well into the nights and weekends, barely keeping their heads above water. He thought if he could just add another tech specialist, everything would be fine.

Anna called Jelani in to discuss the situation, and immediately surprised him by reporting that the complaints were about the quality of the service, and not the speed of delivery. He wasn't prepared for this information and seemed to be at a loss to know how to solve it. We worked with both to carefully evaluate the situation and discovered that Jelani's feedback system had fallen apart. He had not been providing enough information to those customers waiting for service, and at the same time had not been giving performance feedback to his direct reports who provided the service. The pressing needs had forced everyone's heads down, noses to the grindstone, communication becoming a time-consuming non-necessity—so they thought.

Anna and Jelani continued to work together to improve performance. They crafted a careful plan to facilitate changes, Anna keeping Jelani accountable and providing honest feedback combined with positive coaching toward a definitive goal. Anna's model of coaching enabled Jelani to do the same with his team. This process allowed Jelani to shift from being an IT worker to truly becoming the IT leader he was intended to be. He changed his communication protocols and style, then established and maintained a positive feedback coaching process with his team members. Anna provided observant and interested oversight, offering the feedback, coaching and accountability Jelani needed as standards improved. Within a few months, instead of complaints Anna was receiving accolades, which she proudly passed on to Jelani and his newly efficient team.

This case study is an excellent example of what we call a "third generation imprint"—the ultimate goal and achievement of Legacy Leaders.

Anna, as Jelani's boss, not only provided feedback, but delivered it with a careful coaching strategy for Jelani's, and his team's, success. In this way she very directly *(and intentionally)* influenced Jelani's ability to do the same with his team, who would ultimately do the same with their direct reports. This is the true heart of Legacy Leadership—building other leaders who build other leaders, who build other leaders....well, you get the idea.

You might require peak performance, but eventually and undoubtedly there will be those times when someone doesn't perform at the level required. What then? What actions do you take? In every garden some plants thrive, and others become wilted, riddled with bugs or just plain puny. What do you do with those? Most often we do what we can to encourage healthy plants, but eventually the under-performers are removed in order to allow the other plants to flourish. If you do not already have an action plan, carefully consider the potential steps to turn failures into successes. We don't like to use that word—*failure*. But nothing is accomplished when we do not honestly own up to it. A failure can be a springboard to success, if it is handled honestly, intelligently and thoughtfully.

> A failure can be a springboard to success, if it is handled honestly, intelligently and thoughtfully.

A leader or employer also cannot require peak performance unless he or she has provided the tools and resources needed to produce that performance. Every employee is provided with the right tools to do his or her job. These tools can include everything from material goods to specialized implements, information and timelines, training and development. Beyond this, however, there is another resource often overlooked: personal support. Support borders the area of Legacy

Practice 3 (Influencing Inspiration and Leadership), but is also addressed here as an "appropriate resource." Legacy Leaders show interest and care for the development of their employees by providing support, appropriate coaching, and other "growth resources." A tiny seed might sprout if it inadvertently falls into the soil. And a row of corn seeds planted meticulously in a garden will most likely yield a lovely row of seedlings. Either way, these tender shoots won't survive without certain resources and continued support. The garden that is weeded, watered, fed and carefully tended will produce abundant harvest. It's the same with people.

Give serious thought to what resources are appropriate for your team members. Make a list to include everything necessary in order for them to not only fulfill, but actually exceed their responsibilities. Ask each person what they need to do his or her job. Make a return commitment to your employees by providing all these things in adequate measure. Beyond the resources and tools, reflect also on what *personal* support for your team members is needed to ensure their success in current positions, their continued success and development, and how you will mentor them for this future success.

And What About You?_____

When schooling leaders on requiring peak performance, we tend to overlook the leader and leap directly to those being led. Once again, accountability and responsibility are not one-way streets. We cannot require peak performance in others, until we require it in ourselves—and hold ourselves just as accountable and responsible as every other member of the organizational team. In some workplaces, the leader's performance is measured and held accountable by the employees, as well as the leader holding employees accountable. It is a *mutual* accountability (calibration) process, which ensures that all members of the team are functioning at their best and everyone has buy-in to performance goals. Perhaps if all organizations were run in this manner we would not encounter as many disturbing business bungles and debacles. Mutual calibration of responsibility and accountability yields a finely tuned instrument, not subject to frequent breakdown or discordance.

The Legacy Leader has clearly defined personal and professional accountabilities, which means first knowing the vision and the goals, then knowing what it takes to satisfy them, and finally and most importantly for this Legacy Practice, knowing how you are accountable for them. Personal accountabilities are those goals and vision which you have determined desirable for you personally, outside those of the organization. Personal accountability involves knowing who you are, your personal values and motivators, your goals, dreams and desires and your individual responsibilities and accountabilities in your business position. This, of course, assumes you *have* personal accountabilities. It is surprising how many people are stumped when asked to delineate theirs. They haven't given the subject much thought. Personal accountability means behaving in ways true to self, and true to the organization or others you serve. A leader who demonstrates personal accountability is aware of self, confident and sure in what he or she believes and does. Not cocky or arrogant, just sure. There is a big difference.

> Personal accountability means behaving in ways true to self, and true to the organization or others you serve.

We assume that you are well aware of your organization's vision and goals. We also assume that you know what it takes to successfully achieve them. Having clearly defined organizational accountabilities, however, involves another two-fold step—*knowing how* you are accountable for them, and then *being* accountable. It requires full awareness of what you are accountable *for* and whom you are accountable *to*, and expects you to accept responsibility for your part of the mess, as well as your part in the success.

There is one more issue great leaders, leaders living legacy, should also carefully consider. Too often we are satisfied if we merely meet stated expectations, even if they fall below our abilities. Is our accountability only to what others expect? What about what we expect of ourselves, knowing our abilities? Legacy Leaders hold themselves accountable for excellence above expectation.

Keep Your Finger in the Wind

Earlier we discussed the importance of having your "finger on the pulse" of your organization at all times. This alone is not enough, however. You must also have your finger on the pulse of the *world at large*—your competition, technology, global trends, politics, economics and just about every other indicator of trends that may affect your business results. Leading with legacy includes being alert to trends that could potentially affect results, and re-calibrating action plans where and when necessary.

An international manufacturer of food preparation equipment specialized in servicing the fast food industry.

This company was privately owned, and the owner was partial to one particular very popular and internationally known fast food restaurant. For several years this manufacturer catered, so to speak, to this one fast food chain, providing all their standard kitchen equipment. The owner was interested only in partnering with this single client chain, thinking the company would be prosperous forever with this "golden egg" customer. Other employees had urged the owner to branch out, to market to other organizations and expand their product line, but such pleas fell on deaf ears. The money was coming in, production was up, and the relationship and future appeared rosy. There was no need to think about broadening their client or product base.

But then, very unexpectedly, at least for these players, a global trend in food consumption changed everything. It seemed that the world was rethinking how and what it ate. The greasy fast food we had consumed for so long was now linked to dire health issues, and the world was paying attention. We became more health conscious, and more aware of what we were putting into our bodies. Thus was born the age of health food. This trend was not sudden, but it became a critical issue almost overnight to this manufacturer and to his client. A chain reaction of sorts caught everyone unprepared. The client fast food chain didn't pay attention to the trends (or they didn't take them seriously), so they didn't plan in advance to alter menus and rethink their kitchen equipment needs. This in turn also blinded the manufacturing company to growing trends in food service. At a particular point in time, it became glaringly obvious that the food chain would have to offer healthier food, prepared on different equipment—and do it now—if it didn't want to fall from its throne as the premiere fast food provider throughout the world. Orders for the old food service equipment came to a screeching halt. The manufacturer was stunned and caught completely off guard. This was a financially devastating and almost fatal blow.

We are pleased to report, however, that due to some fancy footwork, brilliant engineering and marketing, lots of scrambling and very fast reaction times, this manufacturer was able to get past some very questionable months of survival mode operations and emerge again as a top provider of food service equipment—this time with a much broader product line and client base. This owner will never again limit himself to one client with one set of products, and he will be watching trends with an eagle eye. He also will be listening to his employees more. But not all companies can react this quickly, or recover completely from this kind of trend-induced calamity. Many will just disappear.

> **Business trends are the winds that carry necessary change for survival.**

Business trends are the winds that carry necessary change for survival. Do you test the winds and soar with changes, or is your leadership more like an ostrich than an eagle? Sometimes trends and "indicators" can force us into the process of re-calibration, desired or not. This can be called *re*-active calibration if we wait to act until there are no other options. Being alert to trends, however, enables *pro*-active calibration, which allows forward progress without the need to stop and change gears. Changes can be made while still in motion, while the bottom line is still healthy, and this can quite literally make the difference between survival and extinction in this rapidly changing business environment.

Great leaders have a strong internal focus in order to keep their businesses running smoothly and effectively. But this cannot be at the expense of an equally strong external focus. The world today changes quickly, and without a real-time awareness of these changes, businesses will fall by the wayside as victims of the ostrich syndrome. The first thing that comes to mind when we think of ostriches is their apparent odd behavior when sensing danger—sticking their heads in holes in the ground. It is interesting to note, however, that this behavior has never been observed in ostriches. It is attributed to a myth originated by Pliny the Elder, a first century A.D. Roman writer of natural history. But other characteristics still make the ostrich a good mascot for those who ignore trends, or are unaware of them. The ostrich is the largest bird on the planet and can run very fast, but it is unable to get off the ground. It can't fly. Business and world trends can be likened to the thermals that eagles ride to soar to great heights of visibility. It would take a hurricane or tornado to get the ostrich off the ground, and then he would only plummet back to earth.

A Sense of Urgency

Going back to your road map, you have most likely established some time restraints for the trip you intend to take. Modeling urgency for the journey is about setting the pace for a timely trip, "making good time" as we sometimes say while traveling from one place to another. Modeling urgency is *not* about not stopping when you need to. It is about leading your traveling companions in a *steady pursuit* of your goals, as measured against your time commitments, and against the need for change. We have spoken of the necessity to continually check milestones and measure progress, and to keep your finger constantly in the winds of trend and potential change, but the *speed* at which any course changes or critical decisions are made is paramount. A great leader knows when to make certain choices. He or she develops a sense of timing, prioritization and follow-through. Excellence in decision making is a cultivated sense achieved only through a commitment to alertness and promptness in action, with a sense of urgency. Don't misunderstand, however; not every decision must be made immediately, or subsequent action follow such a choice instantaneously. Timing is everything. The Legacy Leader will carefully evaluate a

> A sense of urgency does not always mean immediate action or rushed decisions.

situation or condition, make a well-considered choice, develop action plans, be aware of the big picture, and determine the best time for action. A sense of urgency does not always mean immediate action or rushed decisions. And it doesn't always mean change. Sometimes staying the course is the correct action, and this also requires a sense of urgency in knowing when to make these critical decisions. Timing is critical, but several other factors are to be considered, and questions answered:

1. What situation prompted the need for change? (i.e., why change?)

2. Is change really needed?

3. What, exactly, is the change needed?

4. How will this change satisfy the perceived need?

5. What actions are required to satisfy the need for the change? How could these actions even exceed, not just meet, the need?

6. What will happen if no change is made?

7. What will happen if the change is made?

8. How will this change affect the whole picture (other departments, other people, the bottom line)?

9. What time constraints are present for this change?

10. How will timing affect the action selected, and overall results of the change?

Richard was the founder and leader of a company that began small, but had grown to a sizable organization over the years.

His health was failing, and he needed to seriously consider retirement. Fortunately, Richard's son Frank had grown up with the business and was preparing to step into his father's shoes and take the helm. Frank's generation viewed things differently than his father's, however, and Frank was more aware of some growing changes in their industry. As he viewed the statistics about changing demographics, aging baby boomers, and the way the younger generation viewed and bought any kind of product, including their service, Frank realized that not only would he have to step up and into the leadership of the company, he was also going to have to respond quickly—urgently—to these industry challenges. Richard didn't see the need to change, and didn't want to pursue any major "reinventions" as he saw them. The way the company worked now was good enough all these years. Yet Frank persisted, and modeled a sense of urgency to employees. The service world had been coming to this tipping point for years, but as long as they were still making money, companies didn't need to look at making changes.

Frank knew he couldn't ignore the obvious, however, and he couldn't put off any longer major retooling of the entire organization. And that's just what Frank launched. Studies showed the younger generation was Internet-dependent, and preferred having 24/7 access worldwide to handle their service needs, rather than the old-school approach of a face-to-face paper and pencil, slower-moving relationship. Employees and consultants scurried to make changes in every system, including marketing and sales approaches, a new sales commission structure and new recruiting procedures. Frank's group quickly turned this aging organization into a dynamic new and agile company with a youthful look, multiple sales pathways, and multiple services. Their timing was perfect. As Frank takes on the CEO role, he has rebuilt the company to emerge as an industry leader, well ahead of the competition just now awakening to the need for change.

> **Business death is certain if the leader has not developed this sense of urgency in leading and responding to change.**

Knowing *"when to hold them and when to fold them"* is one thing. Responding with a sense of urgency is quite another. We've all heard the saying *"you snooze, you lose."* Some say that for leaders, this needs to be a "sixth" sense—it is mandatory. In order to survive a world where change is inevitable, and increasing daily, the leader of tomorrow is alert, flexible, and urgently agile in his or her response to change and possible chaos.

Leadership issues are complex, kept in motion by a constant need for change. Increasing technology, economic issues, down-sizing, expansion, regulatory requirements, competition, world wide opportunities and many other factors make change just as certain as the proverbial death and taxes. Business death is certain if the leader has not developed this sense of urgency in leading and responding to change.

The Bottom Line

Calibrating responsibility and accountability is making sure that the aim of the arrow is true, that the desired "bull's eye" is achieved. We hold vision and values when the arrow is aimed (Legacy Practice 1) and we calibrate responsibility and accountability when we go through the careful steps of learned marksmanship as the arrow is launched. After the launch, however, we do not turn away to shoot again without carefully examining the impact point. That examination is either a celebration of hitting the mark, or an analysis of wayward missiles. A calibrator measures what is, and makes alterations to achieve what is desired. Calibration is not discipline. Discipline involves rigid rules and punishment. Calibration of responsibility and accountability provides guidance, direction, careful correction, consistent growth and celebration of success. However, the end does not justify the means if vision and values are compromised. The means—the process—is the focus here. How we have conducted ourselves on the process road to the "end" is what is justified, and kept accountable, and is ultimately what ensures our success.

Legacy
Practices
1 and 5
are the
"bookends"
of Legacy
Leadership.

This Legacy Practice is all about execution and performance, making sure that aim is correct and the arrow hits the mark. It is a performance process that is trackable, reportable, and explainable for future reference and current success. Responsibility and accountability are often sadly lacking both in individual and corporate presence. That may be simply because we don't know where to begin. Legacy Leaders who practice calibrating responsibility and accountability learn how to communicate, with clarity, expectations, milestones, and methods of measurement—then follow up with appropriate corrective or celebratory action, not mere lip service or a blind eye. We look at this Legacy Practice as the "bookend" to the first practice discussed in this book. Practices 1 and 5 hold everything else together. Holding vision and values is one bookend holding the leadership model together, but all the "books" will topple if the other bookend, calibrating responsibility and accountability, is not firmly in place. This last Legacy Practice will create a path to a deliberate process with a desired outcome.

Reflection

1. How are you effectively applying, and living, Legacy Practice 5: Calibrating Responsibility and Accountability for leadership legacy?

2. What plan do you have in place to make corrections and adjustments if you have discovered that you are not in alignment with your stated performance indicators?

3. What specific areas would you like to develop pertaining to this Legacy Practice?

Next Steps

Are you ready to become a true calibrator, and ensure that all your leadership efforts are hitting the mark for success? Use the Development Guide at the back of this book to get started:

a) The **10 Critical Success Skills:** Core Competencies for Legacy Practice 5
b) **Consideration:** Professional Development *(Questions to guide your development as a Calibrator of Responsibility and Accountability)*

5

c) **Essence:** Being a Legacy Leader *(The BE-Attitudes of the Calibrator of Responsibility and Accountability)*

d) **Application:** Putting it to Work *(Steps for applying Legacy Practice 5)*

e) **Legacy Shifts:** Expected Outcomes
(Shifts in behavior and environment that can be expected as a result of applying this Legacy Practice)

The Development Guide for Legacy Practice 5 begins on page 265. Apply what you have just read to create a path to deliberate and desired success.

EPILOGUE: Pulling It All Together

When you attend a symphony,
ballet or musical production of any kind,
arriving early is always an adventure in
musical cacophony. The early birds are treated to
a preview of the production score as the orchestra
practices and tunes up.

For the listener, the only problem with this practice session is the fact that each musician is playing random snatches of the production, and is not in sync with the rest of the orchestra. The resulting noise is just that—noise. We hear the winds, the brasses, the strings and the resounding kettle drums, but so far they are merely making noise, not music. At a golden moment silence captures our attention as the conductor takes the stage. What was once nothing more than random notes and clashing sounds suddenly becomes sweet and savory blends of melodic harmony.

Legacy Leading

As you have progressed through this book, we may compare your learning to an orchestra. Each Legacy Practice is like a section of instruments warming up. Legacy Leadership is a symphony played on many instruments. We have taken you through the five Legacy Practices and their corresponding critical success skills. There are many "instruments" that will contribute their functional parts to the whole of this orchestra. All of them are required to enjoy the fullness of sound for this symphony of leadership, and all will need the direction and oversight of the conductor to make music, not noise. *You* are the conductor of this orchestra. You set the pace, you tap the podium and you instruct and guide the pieces to function as a whole.

> Legacy Leadership requires *living* today the behaviors, competencies and attitudes of the great leader who will be remembered tomorrow.

The unique part about *this* orchestra, though, is that you also play all the instruments. To make "leadership *music*," the kind that is remembered and influences great composers of the future, you need to play each instrument *well*—and in company with all the others. Quite simply, Legacy Leadership requires that all five Legacy Practices, and all of their associated critical success skills, become integrated, harmonious parts of the leader's repertoire of leadership.

Like music, leadership requires practice. To be a *professional* musician, or a Legacy Leader, requires more than practice. Professional musicians eat, sleep and live their art form and their music. So it is with leadership. A leader does not become a leader when he or she enters the revolving doors of the business venue, and ceases to be that leader upon exiting. When a musician leaves the stage, he or she is still a musician. We have heard stories of professional musicians who actually rehearse in their sleep, or find themselves "playing" their chosen instruments in a kind of mental virtual reality, while performing other seemingly unrelated and mundane physical chores. Legacy Leadership requires *living* today the behaviors, competencies and attitudes of the great leader who will be remembered tomorrow—not just in the workplace, but everyplace. And like the musician, you will need to know, believe and do this leadership wherever you are, living the entire score as it becomes a natural extension of who you are.

Legacy Living

Leadership is not limited to business. While we most often equate leadership with business, the greatest leaders in history—those with the most *legacy*—have often come from other environments. Leaders exist in education, government, military, non profit organizations, and even the home, just to name a few. Wherever there are people interacting together, there are leaders. And the same qualities and competencies that define a great business leader, also define leaders of all kinds, in all places. Leadership is leadership, regardless of where it is practiced, or who is being led. Legacy Leadership is easily adapted to any of a long list of leadership venues. While this current model features some business-specific language, it translates quite easily across other environments, platforms and leadership systems. Are you a father or mother, a teacher or student, a youth director or non-profit organizer? This model fits your leadership needs. We have adapted Legacy Leadership to a variety of other leadership systems, and so can you. A great business leader is most likely also a great Cub Scout or Brownie leader. A Legacy Leader within a corporation is generally also a *legacy* parent, a *legacy* teacher or a *legacy* volunteer and community member. We call this *legacy living*, and it is one of the basic underlying concepts of this leadership model—it works everywhere. We encourage those who are truly interested in becoming Legacy Leaders to begin applying these skills to every area of leadership, beginning at home. *Live* your legacy of leadership wherever you are. Try translating the business language of this model into the living language of your non-business environment. It's not difficult. Then put the model to work for you as you lead others—any time, and in any place.

> The five Legacy Practices reflect the core being
> of great leaders. They are holders, creators,
> influencers, advocators and calibrators.

This *being* may be translated into a 5-step process for the *doing* of Legacy Leadership as a whole, helpful in understanding and applying the holistic approach of Legacy Leadership.

Step 1. **HOLD** it

You may find it very useful to go back and re-read this book—and keep re-reading it. The first Legacy Practice addresses the *being* of the leader in the area of vision and values. This leader is a holder who first *knows*, then *embraces, encourages* and *lives* the vision. Your vision as a leader is not just whatever vision is promoted by your organization, but the *vision you have of yourself as a leader.* Legacy Leadership contains the complete structure and framework around which you can build great leadership. If this is your vision, then you need to know it before you can embrace it. Just like the architect and builders who carry and reference blueprints and plans for whatever structure they are building, you will hold this leadership system as a standard and guide for building your leadership. Use this book as a field guide, a well-worn handbook that enables you to identify the practices that will set you apart as a leader among leaders. After you have become comfortable and very familiar with these concepts, then you can begin to integrate them into your leadership being, embrace them as you actively *be* the leader you want to be remembered for, and encourage their practice in other individuals and organizations. It is first familiar, and personal, before becoming legacy.

Step 2. **CREATE** it

A Legacy Leader is a creator of opportunity. Be alert to open doors where you can create opportunities to not only use and model Legacy Leadership, but also encourage it in others. The second Legacy Practice is about creating opportunities for collaboration and innovation. This collaborative process is part of your overall leadership practice. You are creating opportunity not only for others to collaborate and innovate, but also for yourself as you interact with those you lead. The sports or talent scout is constantly sniffing the air for opportunity, an ear to the ground and a finger in the air to enable the detection of possibility, and the chance to create innovative potential. Leadership is a dance—but not a solo performance. It is intricately interwoven with the movements of others. While most professional dancers are carefully choreographed to work together, leadership requires spontaneity, and alertness to impromptu opportunity for improvement. It calls for the leader to be nimble, flexible, aware—and creative. Your tools for creating legacy as a leader are the five Legacy Practices and the associated critical success skills. With practice, you will begin to see more and more potential to create opportunities to master these skills, and to actively become the creator of your own great leadership.

Step 3. **INFLUENCE** it _____

In Legacy Practice 3, we have defined an influencer as one who brings about a desired effect in others. While most of us have mentors and great influencers in our lives, *we* are inarguably the greatest influencer of our own futures. The flight instructor will transfer knowledge about the airplane, weather conditions, controls and all the other nuances of flying, and even fly as co-pilot during initial student flights. Eventually, however, the student flies solo, becoming a fully trained pilot, responsible now for his or her own knowledge and decisions. Others may contribute to shaping who we are. Ultimately, however, *we* make the personal decisions that influence what we end up being. It may sound a little awkward at first, but we need to get used to the idea that we influence ourselves more than any one else does. As the saying goes, we are the captains of our own ships. The winds and waves may influence movement somewhat, but our combined resources of ability, knowledge and commitment will determine where the ship goes, and even if it stays afloat. It is critical for the person who intends to be a Legacy Leader to make a commitment to the process, and continue to influence that process by making right choices and informed decisions. This is accomplished by honing abilities and competencies, becoming a student of leadership committed to continuing a lifelong learning process, and actively *selecting* the kinds of positive influences that will help build legacy into your leadership.

> It is critical for the person who intends to be a *Legacy* Leader to make a commitment to the process.

It also means recognizing and eliminating the negative influencers, whether they exist on the outside, or on the inside—those that reside in you personally. We all have those inner challenges that may hinder our progress towards legacy—and no one will become a master of all the critical success skills without room for improvement. However, we do not subscribe to the popular philosophy that we just acknowledge our challenges and move on. It is true that some personal weaknesses or challenges are not changeable. For the most part, however, the remainder can be addressed and transformed from a challenge to a strength. But that takes humility and dedicated work. Are you that kind of leader? A Legacy Leader will choose to influence him- or herself in ways that build strengths and even renovate character. What will influence you *to be a Legacy Leader*? What will not?

Step 4. **ADVOCATE** it

The fourth Legacy Practice speaks of being an advocator, one who supports causes, practices and people, standing on their behalf. After reading through this book, have you determined that being a Legacy Leader is what you desire? If it is, then advocate it! That means supporting it in yourself, and in others. It becomes your standard for behavior and your spoken and modeled creed of leadership. You take a stand on leadership, and stick to it. You promote being and doing in ways that support this stand—essentially your leadership position. The Legacy Leader is like the school principal in our comparison analogy, advocating for individuals and whole communities, taking a stand and living it out everyday, everywhere. Likewise, this leader also advocates for his or her own leadership, taking a stand for greatness, living out every detail and competency. Political parties and platforms advocate their causes. Every decision made, every action taken is based upon strict "party" lines. It is meaningless to merely adopt a label, without advocating, and living, certain beliefs, behaviors and lifestyles. Those who wear labels without the accompanying observable life of proofs are hypocrites. So it is for the Legacy Leader. Whether speaking of political parties or leadership, adherents advocate their beliefs and live lives that proves who they are, and it begins by taking a stand that enables you to keep standing through the hurricane force winds of changing thought. Legacy Leadership is timeless, not based on transitional philosophies or trendy ideas, but on what has worked in leadership dynamics throughout human history. If this is the kind of leadership you want, and the kind of leader you want to be, take that stand, and keep standing. Advocate it in your life, and reveal it to others by being and doing what you profess—consistently.

Step 5. **CALIBRATE** it

You recall the illustration of the piano tuner for the fifth Legacy Practice. Without constant attention, and prompt adjustment to even one key out of tune, it wouldn't matter if you were playing Beethoven's Ninth or "Chopsticks"—it all sounds terrible. We don't hear the intended beauty of the composition, only the one discordant note that keeps assaulting our ears. In an orchestra, one instrument not tuned correctly spells disaster. Likewise, in leadership, even one area of competency or practice not calibrated correctly can portend the leader's demise. The Legacy Leader keeps calibrating, keeps tuning, his or her own leadership competencies, behaviors and attitudes. In this fifth Legacy Practice of calibrating responsibility and accountability, the focus was primarily on the leader calibrating—adjusting—the conditions, environment and actions in his or her area of responsibility. By far the greatest area of responsibility for the Legacy Leader, however, is the personal one. Your greatest responsibility and accountability lies in self-calibration, the adjusting and tuning of your own leadership so that the symphony is remarkable and memorable, not known for its "clinkers" but its consistent excellence. Without this constant sense of calibration *(akin to a computer antivirus program that runs automatically in the background of leadership)*, the leader has no ability, and no right, to calibrate or adjust anything else. Develop and practice (until automatic!) a process of leadership self-calibration.

A Word About Motivation

We believe that if you have read this far in this book, you desire to employ the foundational tenets of Legacy Leadership in order to become a Legacy Leader. At this point, we'd like to ask you a critical question. *Why* do you want to do this? What are your personal motivations for becoming this kind of leader?

We have mentioned several times that this Legacy Leadership is others-centered, not self-centered. The concept of legacy in this model demands that your leadership influences others in a way that shapes *their* leadership competencies and future, not just your own. And, of course, we are anticipating that this is positive influence, not negative. Both positive and negative influence will shape the leaders of tomorrow, one way or another. *Legacy*, in the best sense of the word, however, exalts the positive. Remember that we cannot *not* influence. This model promotes that influence as positive and intentional.

Back to the *why* question. Why do you want to be a Legacy Leader? Is it to build others, or to build yourself? Do you desire this status merely to attain higher leadership levels, and therefore achieve greater financial success? In itself, this isn't a bad motivator, yet to be a true Legacy Leader, it can't be the primary motivator. Legacy Leadership is selfless, desiring to place the interests of others before self-interests. You can employ the stated critical success skills and Legacy Practices without this selfless attitude of leadership, and achieve some level of success. These competencies and practices do define what works. However, if you want to rise to a level that separates mere leaders from Legacy Leaders, your attitude is first others-centered. It's not all about you. It's not all about me. It's about being and doing what benefits others first—giving of self to build others. We have observed that there is an amazing side-effect to this attitude. It is quite interesting what happens when we set aside our egos to allow the growth of others. We grow too, and our leadership strengthens. Teams thrive, and bottom lines swell.

> Do you really want to be a **Legacy** Leader, or just a good leader?

Some have looked at this leadership model and concluded that unless the leader begins with this selfless attitude, or seems to have this attitude inherently, these basics of leadership will go right over the heads of most people. They just don't get it. In some respects that might be true. Unless an individual can approach leadership with this kind of selfless foundation for competencies and skills to reside, he or she will likely not be a Legacy Leader. Legacy Leaders put others first. This is a characteristic of the great leader's core being. Still, we believe in the strength and determination of the human spirit, and the ability of the human creature to change, even at the core of being.

You may be one of those who instantly relates and identifies with this concept of selfless leadership—the heart of Legacy Leadership. You have processed through these skills and can readily see how they would work in application—you just need to familiarize yourself and practice them. If that is true, we have essentially been "preaching to the choir" and enabling it to sound even better, providing guidelines for practice. Perhaps, however, you might be reading these words, and this book, thinking mostly of how it would benefit you, not considering this aspect of being *others*-centered for leadership legacy. And just maybe you have reached this place and something inside you is squirming or resisting a bit, aware that your attitude isn't quite as selfless as this model requires. As we said above, you can adopt these practices and improve your leadership without changing your attitude. You are at a crossroads here, however. Do you really want to be a *Legacy* Leader, or just a good leader? If you want to be a leader with positive and lasting *legacy*, are you willing to change your attitude and *become* what this model advocates? Are you willing to set aside your ego? It all begins with the desire and willingness to change. If you want this, you can *be* it. You *can* change your attitude. We've seen it happen many times, but unflinching desire and dedicated commitment precedes any real change.

Hold the vision and values of what you want to become, *create* opportunities to be that kind of leader, *influence* yourself in ways that promote this attitude, *advocate* this kind of leadership in yourself, and calibrate it—until you become it.

Appendices

ONE: Development Guide

Introduction

Legacy Practice 1:
   Holding Vision and Values

Legacy Practice 2:
   Creating Collaboration and Innovation

Legacy Practice 3:
   Influencing Inspiration and Leadership

Legacy Practice 4:
   Advocating Differences and Community

Legacy Practice 5:
   Calibrating Responsibility and Accountability

TWO: Using This Model

Seasoned Leaders

Emerging Leaders

Organizations

Coaches, Consultants and Other Leadership Specialists

THREE: About the Authors

CoachWorks® International, Inc.

Dr. Jeannine Sandstrom

Dr. Lee Smith

FOUR: Acknowledgements

Appendix
ONE

Development Guide

Contents and Suggested Use of This Guide

a) **Critical Success Skills:** Core Competencies

In order to enhance the practical application of Legacy Leadership, each of the five Legacy Practices also has ten critical success skills. These skills contain the competencies, attitudes and behaviors which are the hallmark of great leaders. There are a total of 50 of these success markers and together they help the leader craft and shape behaviors and attitudes that build leaders of living legacy.

b) **Consideration:** Professional Development

(Questions to guide your development as a Legacy Leader)

Several questions regarding the specific application of this Legacy Practice are presented for your consideration in this section. They are intended to allow you to think on a personal, professional, and organizational level as you begin putting the concepts of this Legacy Practice to work. Not all of these questions will be applicable for you, nor may you even wish to answer them all. We suggest you read through them quickly at first. Some will not apply, but some may capture your attention immediately, causing you to stop and think. That is their function—to prompt you to stop a moment and think about your leadership, and your organization, considering the questions posed and providing honest and thoughtful responses. Select the top three or five questions that you believe have real relevance to your leadership, and which you believe you can honestly address and use to lead more intentionally and effectively. Considering these questions and your responses is helpful, and for the greatest impact on your leadership we suggest you commit your answers to paper for a more lasting effect.

Obviously we have not allowed enough room in this book for you to completely write out your thoughts. Use a journal to fully elaborate your considerations and plan for development. You may wish to enter bullet lists or one- or two-sentence responses in the space provided, to serve as reminders.

c) **Essence:** Being a Legacy Leader
(The BE-Attitudes of the Legacy Leader)

We speak often in this book about the importance of *being* a leader, not just *doing*. Being a Legacy Leader is not just about doing Legacy Leadership. In this section, which we have entitled the "BE-Attitudes" of Legacy Leaders, we will present several core attitudes, characteristics and values that define

Customize the Development Guide for your own professional and personal use. Not everything will apply, yet some will immediately grab your attention.

the Legacy Leader in that Legacy Practice. The previous section is about *professional* development. This section is about *personal* development. Leadership is not a mere checklist of competencies. It is shaped by who the leader is, his or her core being. While there are many attitudes and characteristics that are necessary for leaders of legacy, we have focused this section on five critical attributes for being a Legacy Leader in each Legacy Practice. Many qualities and attitudes are necessary for good leadership, and we have mentioned some of these. However, this section is intended for *Legacy* Leaders. Not just good, but *legacy* living leaders. For the purposes of these exercises then, we are limiting attention to what we have determined are the most important foundational attributes (core being) to each Legacy Practice. You may wish to add to the lists, and we encourage you to do that at your option, and even to extend these exercises to cover other attitudes on which you may desire to focus your development work. The qualities listed are not intended to be completely exhaustive or all-inclusive of a Legacy Leader's essence. It is just the beginning. Brief definitions for each of the five listed BE-Attitudes are provided, along with the opportunity for you to do a self-assessment in these core characteristics. This is followed by some suggested methods and practices which should help you develop your Legacy Leader BE-Attitudes.

e) **Application**: Putting it to Work
(Legacy Steps for applying the Legacy Practice)
Now we get to the legs of Legacy Leadership. This is the *doing* part of leadership, which follows the *being* part. Each Legacy Practice is separated into its two "doing" components, and several suggested steps are provided for each factor, to implement this Legacy Practice into your leadership. Taken together, they serve as a step-by-step plan of action to leadership with legacy.

f) **Legacy Shifts:** Expected Outcomes
(Shifts in behavior and environment that can be expected as a result of applying this Legacy Practice)
Leaders who begin to practice Legacy Leadership will observe shifts—changes in behavior, attitude and entire environments. These are to be expected, and are what separate the Legacy Leader from other leaders, and his or her organization from other organizations. In this section we present Legacy Leadership's expected outcomes. There are no exercises in this part, except to anticipate what can be seen as a result of living your leadership legacy. We present two ends of a spectrum of conditions, and relate them as a shift from one end to the other. As you review these expected outcomes, you and

your organization will most likely not align with either end (the extreme "low" or the extreme "high" end). The higher range of the continuum is the ultimate goal, the expected outcome. As a mental exercise, you might try marking yourself or your organization on an imaginary line between these two conditions. A Legacy Leader can expect to see outcomes that peg to the right on your scale.

This Development Guide was designed to take you from a place of knowledge to a place of implementation and action plans with expected outcomes. Even well before you get to the Development Guide, we anticipate you will be considering how these concepts will have real application to your leadership. The guide is provided as a structured way to help you implement your plans.

There are many leaders in our world. Those who desire to grow their core being and competencies will be the most successful, influential and effective leaders; and more important, leaders whom people desire to follow—*Legacy* Leaders.

Legacy Practice 1

HOLDING VISION AND VALUES

Critical Success Skills: Core Competencies

Holding Vision and Values involves an unswerving commitment to intentional behavior that enables an organization to realize its vision and operate with integrity—consistently. These behaviors are not mere references to non-measurable goals or giving lip service to a stated code of ethics. A Legacy Leader embraces and practices ten critical success skills which serve to shift entire organizational cultures to realize goals, and doing so also provides a solid leadership model for tomorrow's leaders. The success skills for this first Legacy Practice will always be hallmarks of great leaders.

1. Consistently reinforce organizational vision and values.
2. Intentionally model guiding principles in everything, with everyone.
3. Personally integrate organization's vision in all responsibilities.
4. Have a well-defined strategic plan for accomplishing the vision.
5. Enable the team to translate organizational vision, and align daily responsibilities with organizational goals.
6. Establish measurable milestones congruent with vision.
7. Ensure that organizational values are integrated into how the organization does business.

Legacy Practice 1: *DEVELOPMENT GUIDE*

1

8. Clearly identify your personal values; "walk the talk" in everything.

9. Place importance on developing others.

10. Effectively communicate, sustain processes to achieve vision and values.

Consideration: Professional Development

1. Does your organization have a clear, compelling and written statement of vision? If not, what can you do about it?

2. How can you translate the company's vision and strategic plan so that you have complete ownership by each person in your area?

3. For even greater success in meeting corporate vision, can you make personal and professional vision match the company vision? How would this be possible in your area?

4. We have seen how vision is to be wed to strategy, and how strategy is measured with standards and accountabilities. How will your measurement processes ensure the vision is achieved?

5. Does your organization have a set of guiding principles (values)? Does every member of your team know, understand and have commitment to these values?

6. How do these guiding principles affect their behavior—and yours? What is the result of abiding by them—or not? What area-wide (or organizational-wide) accountabilities are in place?

7. What does the complete integration of guiding principles and values look like in your area of responsibility?

8. What will you do, if you determine that the organization's guiding principles have not been integrated, or are not being modeled throughout your area of responsibility? How will you address this issue with your team members, and how will you set accountability in place for this?

9. At this moment, how would you rate yourself, on a scale of 1 to 5 (5 being the highest) as a leader who intentionally develops the potential of others? If you scored yourself a 3 or below, what can you do to bring your rating up to a 5, with your current team members? Try making a plan and list practical steps.

10. Based solely upon what you would expect as responses from your team members (*not on your personal opinion*), how effective are you at communicating and sustaining all processes and systems in your area of responsibility?

11. Can you honestly say your area has accomplished the organization's vision and achieved its values? If not, why not? What practical steps can you take to move closer to this goal?

1

Legacy Practice 1: DEVELOPMENT GUIDE

Essence: *Being* a Legacy Leader
The BE-Attitudes of a Holder of Vision and Values

When we attempt to compile lists of the necessary attitudes and qualities of good leaders as they might pertain to this Legacy Practice, we would expect to see such core characteristics as visionary, a communicator, open and not guarded, a role model, and a person of integrity. These would head the list of many other attitudes that could be named here. However, this book is not about just good, or great, leaders. It is about *Legacy* Leaders. Legacy sets these leaders apart from all others. Leaders who live their legacy now will possess certain fundamental attributes and inclinations that enable them to truly lead for legacy as they hold vision and values. We have identified five specific foundational attitudes that distinguish *Legacy* Leaders in this Legacy Practice. These are not listed in any order of importance. Brief descriptions of the top five follow.

A Legacy Leader, a Holder of Vision and Values, IS:

1. **Others-Oriented**
2. **A Guardian**
3. **Seamless**
4. **Values-Driven**
5. **A Whole Systems Thinker**

1. Others-Oriented
This person conducts him or herself in ways that benefit others first, not self. These leaders are aware of other people, their roles, their performance and their needs, and always seek to lift others before self. This leader is sensitive to development opportunities for others. Legacy Leaders are aware of how their personal behavior affects other people and seek to either maximize the positive impact, or minimize the negative.

1

2. A Guardian

This person always <u>protects</u> and <u>champions</u> what is important, such as vision and values, guarding them against erosion or loss, and seeking their incorporation into all behavior and processes.

3. Seamless

This person's <u>life and behavior looks the same regardless of position, place</u> or politics. Business conduct is the same as personal conduct. Public behavior is the same as private behavior. Others cannot detect a change in behavior depending on situation or circumstances.

4. Values-Driven

This person does everything, in all places and positions, based on a personal and professional set of values. These values <u>drive and shape all behavior.</u> This leader is also constantly <u>measuring behavior against values</u>, making correction or changes as necessary.

5. A Whole Systems Thinker

This person has the ability to see life around him or her as a whole system with many parts. This is true in business and general life. These leaders are able to grasp the "big picture" but also understand the many parts that make up that picture. They see the inter-relationships among the parts and how all contribute to the whole.

BE-ATTITUDE SELF ASSESSMENT

How developed is your core being for becoming a Legacy Leader in this Legacy Practice? After reading the descriptions of these BE-Attitudes above, rate yourself *(circle one)* on the following scale, then go on to the steps and questions that follow.

Legacy Practice 1: DEVELOPMENT GUIDE

1

BE-ATTITUDES of a Holder of Vision and Values		RATING: 5=all the time, 0=not at all					
1	I am others-oriented.	5	4	3	2	1	0
2	I am a guardian of what is important.	5	4	3	2	1	0
3	I am seamless in my behavior in all places.	5	4	3	2	1	0
4	I am values-driven.	5	4	3	2	1	0
5	I am a whole systems thinker.	5	4	3	2	1	0

Where do your ratings fall? How many 5's? Any 2's or below? Any zeros?
Here are some suggestions for building the core being of a *legacy* Holder of
Vision and Values.

1. ***Choose your two highest ratings***. Determine how you can leverage
   these strengths to be even more effective in developing and living your
   leadership legacy. ***Also choose two of your lowest*** rating attitudes to be
   your "work on" areas for improvement. Use the questions below to
   build your BE-attitudes.

2. ***Think of someone you know to be this***, to have this attitude, for each of
   the two areas you selected for improvement. For example, if you scored
   yourself low in being seamless in your behavior in all places, who do
   you know whose behavior *is* seamless (past or present)? Identify one
   person for each of the areas you want to develop and do the following
   exercises. Write the attitudes and person's name in the space provided:

   ATTITUDE **PERSON I KNOW WHO DISPLAYS THIS ATTITUDE**

   1.

   2.

Legacy Practice 1: DEVELOPMENT GUIDE

1

Consider the following for each attitude, and person listed:

a. What does this person do that lets me, and others, know he or she is
    _____ (BE-Attitude)?

b. How can I emulate this behavior/attitude?

c. How will this behavior help me become a better leader? A Legacy
    Leader?

3. After completing the above steps, ***make a commitment*** to improve.
    Choose one of your "work on" attitudes each week, and focus on
    improving that attitude in all you think, do and speak.

    a. Be aware of your behavior and thought processes during the week, as
        they pertain to that attitude.

    b. Create a mental reminder that will alert you to old behavior and
        thought patterns you want to change.

    c. When you are alerted to old behavior and thought patterns, change
        them immediately, if possible. If not, use that experience to help
        remind you in the future. Consider what triggered this old behavior
        or attitude, and how you can respond differently in the future.

    d. Evaluate your week for progress and determine how you can improve
        this attitude next week.

Legacy Practice 1: **DEVELOPMENT GUIDE**

1

e. The following week, add another "work on" attitude as your focus, without neglecting the first one.

f. Keep doing this until you notice a definite change (improvement), so that your improved attitude has become part of you, part of your core being as a Legacy Leader. Chances are if *you* notice an improvement, others will as well.

g. If journaling is familiar and comfortable for you, consider keeping track of your BE-Attitude development. Brush away discouragement if things don't change immediately. They will, especially if this is the way you want to be. Sometimes we just need to rethink or reframe how we think and do.

Application: Putting it to Work

Are you ready to fully implement this first Legacy Practice into your leadership? We have provided some practical "Legacy Steps." This is the *doing* part. Be committed and intentional. Practice does make perfect!

Legacy Steps to Holding **VISION**

1. Determine the organization's vision statement(s). If necessary, this may need to be re-stated, re-worked, reaffirmed, or whatever is necessary to provide a clear tool and written communication of the organization's vision.

1

2. Determine how (lay out a plan) you will explain, and communicate this easily to employees and clients.

3. Openly and frequently communicate the vision to all employees at every level, encouraging their buy-in and cooperation.

4. Assure that every decision or action is held up to the organizational vision. Discard those that do not match up.

5. Be sure organizational vision is kept as the foundation of every project and goal until it becomes an automatic "reflex."

6. Be able to easily articulate the organizational (as well as your personal) vision for fellow team members and customers.

7. Formulate personal vision in written and measurable format, and internalize for use in achievement of organizational vision.

8. Bring your whole self to your leadership.

9. Understand that what you do and say today shapes the future, for yourself, and for others.

10. Make the organizational vision compelling, inspiring to others.

Legacy Steps to Holding **VALUES**

1. Determine the organization's values statement(s). If necessary, this may need to be re-stated, re-worked, reaffirmed, or whatever is necessary to provide a clear tool and written communication of your organization's values. How does this company want to be known in the workplace?

Legacy Practice 1: **DEVELOPMENT GUIDE**

1

What values are important? Once values are defined and clearly identified—KNOW them, and live them.

2. Openly and frequently communicate the values to all employees at every level, encouraging their buy-in and cooperation.

3. Assure that every decision or action is measured against organizational values. Discard those that do not match up. No compromise.

4. Be sure organizational values are reflected in every activity so that it becomes an automatic "reflex."

5. Be able to easily articulate the organizational (as well as your personal) values for fellow team members and clients. The talk is important, but remember that the walk is the loudest communicator.

6. Alert team members when particular values may be compromised during any decision making process, or other activity.

7. Avoid self-righteousness.

8. The organization's reputation is your reputation. Consider this when representing your organization to the public or fellow team members.

9. Determine how you might uphold your personal core values if you find that they do not match your organization's values.

10. When mistakes are made, or values compromised, craft a way to acknowledge these, reaffirm values and model holding those values by cleaning up any mess made by the mistake. Avoid "cover-ups."

Legacy Shifts: Expected Outcomes

As you have reviewed this Legacy Practice, you may notice that there are distinctions (or gaps) between where you are now and where you want to be in this practice. Growing in these skills may require shifts of thought and action, and continued practice will produce automatic and natural shifts. These new behaviors and attitudes promote personal leadership development for today, and serve as a foundation for tomorrow's leaders. Practicing these skills will shift the leader, and the organizational culture and environment from growth-retarding to success-stimulating. They also serve as patterns for what the optimal internal business climate looks like, shifting the culture:

FROM fuzzy...**TO focused**

Instead of a team with fuzzy, uncommunicated, and poorly stated vision and goals, each individual is empowered with a clear understanding of organizational vision, allowing them to work in a focused and targeted manner.

FROM wandering lost...**TO following roadmaps and milestones**

Instead of employees wandering through their activities with no apparent strategy, hoping to meet unstated goals, individuals are given clear roadmaps and stated milestones along the way, with consistent guidance in "map-reading" skills.

FROM no personal direction...**TO well-defined vision and goals**

Employees who previously had no personal vision are encouraged to define their own goals and use them to drive their personal and corporate contribution to the organizational vision.

Legacy Practice 1: **DEVELOPMENT GUIDE**

1

FROM lack of policies...**TO well-known guiding principles**

Instead of individuals performing in random and occasionally "out of bounds" methods, all behavior is guided by consistent and well-communicated values.

FROM bad or no reputation...**TO reputation for excellence**

Instead of an organization about which only unfavorable or missing reputation is available (inside or outside the organization), the organization begins to be a "name brand" based on reputation for excellence in all phases of operation and performance. A Legacy Leader's company's branding is noteworthy and respected.

FROM cover-ups...**TO open pride**

Instead of constantly "covering up" behavior or performance that is below the level of acceptable business ethics and values, individuals, teams and leadership begin to take pride and ownership in an organization that holds values as priorities, in consistent and illuminating ways. This behavior spreads from the organizational level to every employee.

1

NOTES

Use this space to jot down any thoughts you might have about your legacy development. Consider referencing this Development Guide, and your notes, on a regular basis in the future.

Legacy Practice 2

CREATING COLLABORATION AND INNOVATION

Critical Success Skills: Core Competencies

The ten critical success skills that build legacy around this practice involve certain behaviors that advance the mere concepts of collaboration and innovation to the place where the leader is responsible for actively and intentionally creating these opportunities. To create *collaboration* within an organization, the Legacy Leader ensures high levels of trust, develops processes for building and capturing the collaboration, and encourages a team spirit. Creating *innovation* relies first on the collaborative process, then on a creative environment that challenges new thought, without boundaries.

1. Create innovative and sound possibilities for the organization.
2. Foster a learning, trusting environment for true collaboration and innovation.
3. Masterfully listen for both what is said and not said.
4. Be comfortable not knowing "the answers" and learn from individual perspectives.
5. Draw out differing perspectives and believe disagreement is a learning opportunity.
6. Ask timely, tough questions while keeping in mind the big picture.
7. Set the tone for thinking beyond the present in order to innovate for the future.

8. Project how ideas will play out in the organization and in the marketplace.

9. Discern, and assist others to understand, when change needs to happen and when it does not.

10. Masterfully facilitate conversations where everyone contributes best thinking toward task/goal.

2

Consideration: Professional Development

1. List at least three ideas you have had in the past three months to improve either your personal work responsibilities, or the functions within your area of responsibility. Jot them down in a table with three columns (like the one below): idea, created possibility, and status. What is the idea, what have you done to create a possibility for this idea to work or be implemented, and what is the current status? How have you taken your ideas and turned them into possibilities? What was the result? What ideas have your team members brought to you, and what did you do with them?

Ideas	Possibilities?	Status?

2. What criteria needs to be met to determine if your ideas are innovative and sound? Look back at the list of ideas you created above. Single out one or two which have not yet been realized. List at least five questions or criteria to determine the innovation and soundness of your ideas. Do you routinely screen ideas by these criteria? How, when, and what is the result? What factors do you need to consider that impact the organization as a whole?

3. How are you creating an environment where people *want* to create ideas?

4. How would you describe your listening abilities? Do you "practice" listening well? Is this part of your leadership style? What advantages are there to you, and to your organization, when you listen masterfully? How does listening masterfully enhance collaboration? Do you, and your organization, place a high value on meaningful dialogue?

5. Think of a time when someone seriously questioned you, on either a personal or professional level, that caused you to really evaluate your responses, and may have even enabled you to re-think your position or direction. What kinds of questions were asked of you, and *how* were they asked? What made the difference in your responses and the outcome? Now consider a business meeting when perhaps a leader (*or you*) did not ask either the obvious or deeper level questions that needed to be asked. What was the result? Why do you think those questions weren't asked? What could have been done differently?

2

Legacy Practice 2: **DEVELOPMENT GUIDE**

6. How can you improve, and how can you ensure, a more collaborative learning environment in your area of responsibility, and throughout the organization? How might this contribute significantly to innovation?

7. Do you effectively draw out differing perspectives from your team members? How? What do you do with these ideas?

8. Recall a recent incident involving disagreement between you and your team members. How was it handled? What was the result? Was something new learned? Did it lead to collaboration and innovation, or to some less desirable conclusion? What could you have done differently? How can *you*, as the leader in your area of responsibility, turn disagreement into powerful and innovative collaboration?

9. How much time and thought do you regularly give to the future of your functional area, as well as the future of the organization? How do you translate this to your team members? Do you set the tone for their thinking, as well as your own? How do you maintain balance with the present and the future?

10. Do you regularly encourage your team members to be innovative and collaborative regarding the future? How do you do this? What is the result? How can you improve?

11. How do you create the environment for collaborative innovation for the future or your organization?

12. Have you tested your ability to successfully predict and project the success of ideas within the organization or marketplace? How do you do that, and what has been the result? How do you rate your ability as a "prognosticator?" How can you improve your ability to project ideas successfully? Try listing at least three concrete steps you can take right now to test these ideas.

13. What has been your "track record" for discerning the need for change? Think carefully about this and try to describe those times. How can you improve this ability?

14. Does change really need to occur? Do you know it needs to occur? Do your team members know it? How do you effectively communicate the need for change? Change always involves others. Do you always consider how change will affect both outcomes and processes to achieve the outcomes? Do you consider how team members and others will be changed? Is change something you do with others?

15. What is the difference between "holding court" and facilitating interaction in your team meetings? How do the results differ? How do you set the tone, what attitudes do you adopt and what actions do you take as a facilitator in these meetings? Do you consider yourself a "masterful facilitator" of conversation?

Legacy Practice 2: **DEVELOPMENT GUIDE**

16. How do you set the tone and masterfully facilitate conversations? What is the "tone of the culture" in your area of responsibility? Does everyone contribute his or her best? Why, or why not?

2

Essence: *Being* a Legacy Leader
The BE-Attitudes of a Creator of Collaboration and Innovation

There are many attitudes and core characteristics necessary for all good leaders. For this Legacy Practice, those might include: trustworthy, affirming, sharing, creative, observant, and collaborative, among many others we could list here. To achieve greatness, however, a Legacy Leader takes core attitudes to a higher level—more focused, purposeful and conscious, until they are integrated into who this leader is, every day in every place. We have listed attitudes, or qualities, that we consider the Top Five BE-attitudes for your consideration in this Legacy Practice. These are not listed in any order of importance. Brief descriptions follow.

A Legacy Leader, a Creator of Collaboration and Innovation, IS:

1. **A Trust Builder**
2. **An Intuitive Listener**
3. **Possibility-Minded**
4. **"Charge-Neutral"**
5. **Mentally Agile**

1. A Trust Builder

This person always seeks to build trust in relationships. It is an automatic inclination which is composed of and driven by both trustworthiness and a trusting nature. These people have a mind set of connectiveness, and know that trust is built in order to connect firmly with others.

2. An Intuitive Listener

Listening is a core quality for this person, but it is also accompanied with an intuitive and discerning ear. This person desires to hear others, and consciously listens both to what is said, and what is not said. This person can gather an amazing amount of information by listening well and often.

3. Possibility-Minded

This person has developed an automatic reflex which allows them to see possibilities and opportunities, even when others may not. He or she is open-minded, and is able do mental feasibility exercises in almost any situation. This person is approachable, open to innovative thinking, and can thoroughly consider potential favorable possibilities in almost any situation.

4. Charge-Neutral

This is a term used in training coaches to be unbiased, non-judgmental and non-positioned with clients. A person who is charge-neutral has a neutral starting point for all ideas, people and things. This person does not pre-judge anything or anyone, and is open to receive all information (uncensored) before making decisions or judgments.

5. Mentally Agile

This characteristic is not necessarily a function of intelligence, but the ability to think quickly, remain flexible, shift gears as necessary and allow the ebb and flow of ideas to chart courses. This person has the ability to weigh ideas and actions quickly, yet is still able to discern wisely. He or she is also able to track details, and to see both the forest and the trees.

Legacy Practice 2: **DEVELOPMENT GUIDE**

BE-ATTITUDE SELF ASSESSMENT

How developed is your core being for becoming a Legacy Leader in this Legacy Practice? After reading the descriptions of these BE-Attitudes above, rate yourself *(circle one)* on the following scale, then go on to the steps and questions that follow.

2

BE-ATTITUDES of a Creator of Collaboration and Innovation		RATING: 5=all the time, 0=not at all					
1	I am a trust builder.	5	4	3	2	1	0
2	I am an intuitive listener.	5	4	3	2	1	0
3	I am possibility-minded.	5	4	3	2	1	0
4	I am "charge-neutral."	5	4	3	2	1	0
5	I am mentally agile.	5	4	3	2	1	0

Where do your ratings fall? How many 5's? Any 2's or below? Any zeros? Here are some suggestions for building the core being of a Creator of Collaboration and Innovation.

1. *Choose your two highest ratings.* Determine how you can leverage these strengths to be even more effective in developing and living your leadership legacy. *Also choose two of your lowest* rating attitudes to be your "work on" areas for improvement. Use the questions below to build your BE-attitudes.

2. *Think of someone you know to be this*, to have this attitude, for each of the two areas you selected for improvement. For example, if you scored yourself low in being seamless in your behavior in all places, who do you know whose behavior *is* seamless (past or present)? Identify one person for each of the areas you want to develop and do the following exercises. Write the attitudes and person's name in the space provided:

Legacy Practice 2: DEVELOPMENT GUIDE

2

ATTITUDE	PERSON I KNOW WHO DISPLAYS THIS ATTITUDE
1.	
2.	

Consider the following for each attitude, and person listed:

a. What does this person do that lets me, and others, know he or she is
    _____ (BE-Attitude)?

b. How can I emulate this behavior/attitude?

c. How will this behavior help me become a better leader? A Legacy
    Leader?

3. After completing the above steps, ***make a commitment*** to improve.
    Choose one of your "work on" attitudes each week, and focus on
    improving that attitude in all you think, do and speak.

    a. Be aware of your behavior and thought processes during the week, as
        they pertain to that attitude.

    b. Create a mental reminder that will alert you to old behavior and
        thought patterns you want to change.

Legacy Practice 2:   **DEVELOPMENT GUIDE**

2

c. When you are alerted to old behavior and thought patterns, change them immediately, if possible. If not, use that experience to help remind you in the future. Consider what triggered this old behavior or attitude, and how you can respond differently in the future.

d. Evaluate your week for progress and determine how you can improve this attitude next week.

e. The following week, add another "work on" attitude as your focus, without neglecting the first one.

f. Keep doing this until you notice a definite change (improvement), so that your improved attitude has become part of you, part of your core being as a Legacy Leader. Chances are if *you* notice an improvement, others will as well.

g. If journaling is familiar and comfortable for you, consider keeping track of your BE-Attitude development. Brush away discouragement if things don't change immediately. They will, especially if this is the way you want to be. Sometimes we just need to rethink or reframe how we think and do.

Application: **Putting it to Work**

Are you ready to fully implement this second Legacy Practice in your leadership? These practical *"Legacy Steps"* will help you get started. And remember, all the collaboration and innovation in the world are a hollow waste of precious time and resources, unless coupled with action. *Do it!*

Legacy Steps to Creating COLLABORATION

1. Be respectful. Showing respect builds trust.

2. Listen thoroughly. Know what you're talking about before you talk.

3. Honor differences of opinion. Understand how differences can build information.

4. Create an atmosphere where everyone can be heard and feel free to contribute.

5. Encourage everyone's participation. No holdouts!

6. Communicate expectations of collaboration *(what does it look like?)*.

7. Acknowledge equal ranking to all ideas. Set judgment aside. Be open-minded.

8. Focus on the "greater good" of organization, beyond the team framework. (Keep vision and values in sight.)

9. Become familiar with strengths of teammates, perspectives, gifts, points of view, etc.

10. Make interaction fun and invigorating.

11. Speak the truth with respect and clarity.

2

ctice 2:   **DEVELOPMENT GUIDE**

Legacy Steps to Creating INNOVATION

1.   Clearly identify challenge(s).

2.   Gather together a group of cross-functional individuals with unique perspectives and responsibilities.

3.   Clearly establish the process in which you are about to engage. Reaffirm the value of everyone's input.

4.   Set the ground rules. (i.e., no discussion about negative behavior or how "we got into this situation" – no past blaming, only future creating, all ideas worth exploring, think outside box, etc.)

5.   Set up the question: "What do we have to change to have this (goal, vision, etc.) happen?"

6.   Set parameters, boundaries, etc.

7.   Openly work collaboratively to design the process and communication connections to achieve any stated goal.

8.   Do not judge ideas until all innovative thinking is on the table.

9.   All ideas are in writing and all process evaluation is documented, logged for review.

10. Share all ideas, share all processing, share all input/feedback, share in final product.

Legacy Practice 2: **DEVELOPMENT GUIDE**

2

Legacy Shifts: Expected Outcomes

Implementing these competencies and practices will cause dramatic shifts in your work environment, and will produce an attitude of expectation for the future. When you model these behaviors, you are providing a pattern for the next generation of leaders, who will most likely need to "collaborate and innovate" at an even greater level than today. These new behaviors and attitudes promote personal leadership development for today, and a foundation for tomorrow's leaders. When you practice these critical skills and behaviors, you can expect to see some beneficial shifts:

FROM judgment...**TO curiosity**
Instead of judging fellow workers, employees begin wondering what they could accomplish collaboratively.

FROM "ho hum" meetings...**TO "ah hah!" sessions**
Instead of non-productive business as usual meetings, employees anticipate group sessions with expectation for discovery and accomplishment.

FROM suspicion...**TO trust**
Getting to know one another and working collaboratively erases suspicion, the need to protect self and competition, and fosters an environment of trust, critical to collaboration.

FROM ordinary...**TO extraordinary**
Instead of ordinary thinking, team members learn to automatically think beyond to the extraordinary, the unusual, and the innovative.

Legacy Practice 2: **DEVELOPMENT GUIDE**

FROM focus on the past...**TO focus on the future**

Instead of focusing on what has already been, or is being accomplished, a new excitement for the future potential becomes part of innovative thinking.

FROM fear of change...**TO embracing the new**

Instead of fearing change, a human response, employees learn from the behavior of the *Legacy* Leader, that change holds huge potential for exciting new ways to meet goals.

2

NOTES

Use this space to jot down any thoughts you might have about your legacy development. Consider referencing this Development Guide, and your notes, on a regular basis in the future.

Legacy Practice 3

INFLUENCING INSPIRATION AND LEADERSHIP

Critical Success Skills: Core Competencies

Legacy Leaders are trail blazers, forging the path to great leadership with positive influence so that everyone is lifted up to be the best he or she can be. People are invited, not commanded, to contribute from their strengths and are filled with energy to deliver high quality outcomes. This leader is self-inspired, and knows what inspires others. Influencing *inspiration* requires including the heart in all processes, connecting personally with others, and valuing them individually and corporately. To successfully influence *leadership*, the leader makes a conscious choice to be a positive presence that instills confidence rather than destroying it, and actively seeks ways to uplift and enhance the leadership growth of others. The ten critical success skills that compose this best practice include certain behaviors that take inspiration and leadership from mere words on a page to active influencers for shaping corporate success, and tomorrow's leaders, and exchanges organizational command-and-control for a nurturing structure and environment.

1. Be very adept at developing and maintaining relationships.
2. Use emotional intelligence and positive energy to influence others.
3. Choose to model the positive perspective in all situations.

3

Legacy Practice 3: DEVELOPMENT GUIDE

4.   Bring out the best in people.

5.   Constantly acknowledge and recognize the attributes and contributions of others.

6.   Intentionally delegate for the development of others.

7.   Lead with a constant focus on showcasing others, not self.

8.   Have the ability and courage to take risks and inspire others to follow.

9.   Be able to make tough decisions with minimal negative impact.

10. Lead with humility and unwavering resolve to accomplish the goals of the organization through others.

3

Consideration: Professional Development

1.   Think about each of your team members individually. Can you say, honestly, that you care about them and both their personal and organizational success? If so, how do you show it? Are there any in particular with whom you need to work to further develop a caring (and working) relationship? What can you do about those? Can you say that you "understand" your team members as individuals—that is, do you KNOW them, know their abilities, know their challenges and show your understanding? How does understanding your team members help you become more of an influencer?

2.   How do you encourage relationship building in your area of responsibility?

Legacy Practice 3: DEVELOPMENT GUIDE

3. A Legacy Leader chooses to model the positive perspective at all times. Does this describe you—do you make this conscious choice? Why or why not? Think of a specific time when the situation seemed negative, but you were able to approach it with a positive, yet realistic, perspective, yielding positive results.

4. Are you a leader with "warmth?" Do you connect easily with others? How so? Do others see you this way? If not, what can you do about it? How does viewing things with a positive perspective affect your "warmth" rating as a leader?

3

5. Considering what you know about your personal Emotional Intelligence (EI), how does this affect (either positively or negatively) your ability to influence others? What areas of your EI need work? How can you improve them?

6. Does your work reflect positive energy? How? If not, why not? How would you define positive energy in leadership, and more importantly, how do you apply it?

Legacy Practice 3: DEVELOPMENT GUIDE

7. Do you know how to use stories to inspire and influence others to be their best, to communicate in ways that inspire and motivate? Think of an example of a story from your business repertoire, and one about yourself, personally. Have you told these stories to others, and what was the result? If you are not adept at storytelling, what can you, and will you, do about it? Are you willing to learn this skill? Are you willing to share both your successes and your mistakes? Can you think of a situation recently where a good story may have communicated and influenced people more effectively?

3

8. Are you aware of, and have you identified the attributes and contributions of, your team members? Are you *others*-centered enough to be looking for them, to know your team members well enough to know each one? Can you admit they are real and true, and worthy of commendation? (In other words, are you not so lost in self that you can acknowledge the contributions of others?) Do you express appreciation for these attributes and contributions of others? How? Do you formally reward them? How? What is an appropriate reward or acknowledgement and recognition of attributes and contributions among your team members? Think of a specific example of a recent acknowledgement or recognition you gave to one of your team members for his or her attributes or contributions. Here's a difficult question: *Is your heart in this, or is it just for show, to get results?* (Be honest.)

9. How would you describe your delegation skills? Do you delegate for the right reasons? Do you delegate merely to "get the job done," or do you deliberately delegate for the development of others?

10. Can you honestly say that you lead with a constant focus on showcasing others rather than self? Do you desire to "elevate" those around you? Have you made a choice and commitment to do this with your team members?

11. What kind of risk taker are you, especially as it applies to your area of responsibility? Describe your ability and courage on a scale of 1 to 10, with 1 being "milquetoast" and 10 being "ready to leap in the moment." How can you take risks *and* inspire others to follow you on a path of risk and change? What does this look like? Do you do it? What advantage does this behavior have for you, your team members, and your organization?

3

12. How can you, as a role model for everyone in your organization (not just your immediate team members) minimize the negative impact of tough decisions and model behavior that enhances learning and opens doors to opportunity for future success?

Legacy Practice 3:   DEVELOPMENT GUIDE

13. What kind of impact do your decisions have? Do you anticipate and advance the positive and minimize the negative? How do you handle the fallout?

14. Would your team members describe your leadership style as one based on genuine humility? What would they say about you in this regard? Are you satisfied with that? Do you need to make any changes? Can you say that you lead with humility—real humility (not pretense, people know the difference)—always?

3

Essence: *Being* a Legacy Leader
BE-Attitudes of an Influencer of Inspiration and Leadership

Among the long list of qualities and attitudes of a great leader in this Legacy Practice we would expect to find such things as humble, inspirational, others-centered, passionate, and an opportunity seeker (for others), to name just a few.   However, we have already stated that Legacy Leaders have a solid platform of attitudes that set them apart from all other leaders. This leader intentionally influences others through a set of both natural and highly refined basic attitudes that we have delineated for this Legacy Practice. These attitudes mark the very core identity of Legacy Leaders. We have listed the features we consider the Top Five BE-attitudes for your consideration in this Legacy Practice. These are not listed in any order of importance. Brief descriptions follow.

Legacy Practice 3: DEVELOPMENT GUIDE

A Legacy Leader, an Influencer of Inspiration and Leadership, IS:

1. **Relationship-Driven**
2. **Impact-Aware**
3. **Self-Inspired**
4. **A Mentor**
5. **Positive**

1. Relationship-Driven

This person is not just relational, but relationship-driven. This person realizes that everything in life, including business, is driven by relationships and he or she is therefore driven to build and maintain relationships. These people don't just "get along" with people, they must connect with them to thrive.

2. Impact-Aware

This person has developed a discernment that allows them to be consciously aware of surroundings, including his or her own impact on situations and other people. These people understand the value and the responsibility of their impact on other people, and as such are intentional about their influence. They know well the concepts of cause and effect, actions and reactions, and behavior and consequences.

3. Self-Inspired

This person does not need others to inspire self. These people are able to draw personal inspiration from a variety of sources. In this regard they are not externally driven, but self-driven. They are fully aware of what inspires them and are able to seek that inspiration on their own. They are authentic, confident and aware of personal values.

3

Legacy Practice 3: DEVELOPMENT GUIDE

4. A Mentor

This person may or may not have an official role or title as mentor, but they have an inborn attitude of coming alongside others in order to build them and encourage them (mentor-minded). He or she constantly seeks ways to improve others, to develop them, advance them and showcase them. These people have a self-awareness that their own development and experiences may be of benefit to others, and desire to share learning to move others forward.

5. Positive

This person thinks and behaves in positive ways. He or she has an underlying positive viewpoint, and is always searching for (mindful of) the positive avenues and attitudes in any situation. This attitude does not mean this person is not realistic. They are able to think realistically, yet with a positive end point (outcome) in mind.

3

BE-ATTITUDE SELF ASSESSMENT

How developed is your core being for becoming a Legacy Leader in this Legacy Practice? After reading the descriptions of these BE-Attitudes above, rate yourself *(circle one)* on the following scale, then go on to the steps and questions that follow.

	BE-ATTITUDES of an Influencer of Inspiration and Leadership	RATING: 5=all the time, 0=not at all					
1	I am relationship-driven.	5	4	3	2	1	0
2	I am aware of my impact.	5	4	3	2	1	0
3	I am self-inspired.	5	4	3	2	1	0
4	I am mentor-minded.	5	4	3	2	1	0
5	I am positive.	5	4	3	2	1	0

Legacy Practice 3: DEVELOPMENT GUIDE

Where do your ratings fall? How many 5's? Any 2's or below? Any zeros? Here are some suggestions for building the core being of an Influencer of Inspiration and Leadership.

1. ***Choose your two highest ratings.*** Determine how you can leverage these strengths to be even more effective in developing and living your leadership legacy. ***Also choose two of your lowest*** rating attitudes to be your "work on" areas for improvement. Use the questions below to build your BE-attitudes.

2. ***Think of someone you know to be this***, to have this attitude, for each of the two areas you selected for improvement. For example, if you scored yourself low in being seamless in your behavior in all places, who do you know whose behavior *is* seamless (past or present)? Identify one person for each of the areas you want to develop and do the following exercises. Write the attitudes and person's name here:

ATTITUDE **PERSON I KNOW WHO DISPLAYS THIS ATTITUDE**

1.

2.

Consider the following for each attitude, and person listed:

a. What does this person do that lets me, and others, know he or she is _____ (BE-Attitude)?

b. How can I emulate this behavior/attitude?

3

Legacy Practice 3: DEVELOPMENT GUIDE

   c. How will this behavior help me become a better leader? A Legacy
      Leader?

3. After completing the above steps, *make a commitment* to improve.
   Choose one of your "work on" attitudes each week, and focus on
   improving that attitude in all you think, do and speak.

   a. Be aware of your behavior and thought processes during the week, as
      they pertain to that attitude.

   b. Create a mental reminder that will alert you to old behavior and
      thought patterns you want to change.

   c. When you are alerted to old behavior and thought patterns, change
      them immediately, if possible. If not, use that experience to help
      remind you in the future. Consider what triggered this old behavior
      or attitude, and how you can respond differently in the future.

   d. Evaluate your week for progress and determine how you can improve
      this attitude next week.

   e. The following week, add another "work on" attitude as your focus,
      without neglecting the first one.

   f. Keep doing this until you notice a definite change (improvement), so
      that your improved attitude has become part of you, part of your core
      being as a Legacy Leader. Chances are if *you* notice an improvement,
      others will as well.

g. If journaling is familiar and comfortable for you, consider keeping track of your BE-Attitude development. Brush away discouragement if things don't change immediately. They will, especially if this is the way you want to be. Sometimes we just need to rethink or reframe how we think and do.

Application: Putting it to Work

Do you want to be a truly influential leader? The practical *"Legacy Steps"* here will help you start that journey. This Legacy Practice is really a condition of the heart, not necessarily the hands and feet. What we *do* as leaders is merely an extension of who we *are*. Think about that seriously before you begin this process.

3

Legacy Steps to Influencing **INSPIRATION**

1. Develop your ability to successfully influence others to self-motivation and self-inspiration.

2. Discover the strengths of others.

3. Learn what inspires others, and develop an attitude of inspiration.

4. Connect personally with others on all levels.

5. Develop and tell stories (at appropriate times) that inspire.

6. Challenge and encourage others to work from their strengths.

Legacy Practice 3: DEVELOPMENT GUIDE

7. Focus on living a model of consistent inspiration for others.

8. Discard old ideas of motivation. Learn and incorporate a new plan for individual and team inspiration.

9. Continue your own process of learning, and being inspired by others.

10. Learn how to consistently bring out the best in others.

Legacy Steps to Influencing LEADERSHIP

1. Choose to be positive.

2. Open doors, take down walls, and break through any barriers between you and others.

3. Build your knowledge of leadership models and styles. Determine what works and what doesn't. Share info through opportunity and model what works.

4. Work at building the trust of fellow workers.

5. Get to know your team members. Understand their strengths/values/ skills and seek opportunities to encourage use of these gifts to build their leadership acumen.

6. Halt conflict and defuse confrontation with positive energy.

7. Thoroughly and honestly evaluate your leadership intentions and style. Throw out the self-centered and develop the other-centered aspects.

3

8. Respect others—always.

9. Consider everyone you work with a potential leader—then treat them, model for them, and challenge them as such.

10. Take care of yourself holistically. Your well-being will dramatically affect your leadership, and the influence it has over others. Passion and positive energy are directly related to personal well-being, not just professional station.

Legacy Shifts: Expected Outcomes

3

Leaders who adopt and apply these skills and competencies, with an honest and humble heart for others, will experience near-miraculous results. People whom you have labeled negative become positive. Hope displaces frustration and fear of failure. You become a powerful model for the best in leadership and a template for the shaping of future leaders. When you practice these critical skills and behaviors, and even more important, attitudes, you will experience some dramatic, beneficial shifts. This isn't an advertising slogan or empty guess at results. It's a guarantee. These attitudes and behaviors define successful human dynamics. They work.

FROM Heartless...**TO Heartfelt**

Instead of heartless day-to-day grind of expected activity, leaders portray a heartfelt interest in others and a desire to inspire.

Legacy Practice 3: **DEVELOPMENT GUIDE**

FROM Pulling Teeth...**TO Sustained Energy and Passion**

Instead of continually working to generate some type of action, response or specific behavior, leaders inspire others to motivate themselves and provide their own inner energy and known passion.

FROM Bringing Down...**TO Lifting Up**

Motivation and discipline can bring people down and either slow, interrupt or completely stop forward progress. True inspiration lifts others up to heights of clarified "air" and environment which advances and speeds progress.

FROM personal power...**TO empowering others**

Instead of claiming the position as "king" or "queen" of the company or department, the Legacy Leader actively and purposely creates future leaders through consistent modeling of passion and compassion.

FROM a negative attitude...**TO a BE-attitude**

Instead of always seeing the negative, the Legacy Leader actively changes a "bad" attitude to a can be-attitude and a can do-attitude. Attitude is a choice, regardless of the situation. A Legacy Leader deliberately chooses the positive. Soon the choice becomes an automatic reflex.

FROM isolational...**TO relational**

Instead of withdrawing into self-protective shells and behind walls or closed doors, the Legacy Leader deliberately opens doors, establishes relationships and influences others to do the same.

Legacy Practice 3: *DEVELOPMENT GUIDE*

NOTES

Use this space to jot down any thoughts you might have about your legacy development. Consider referencing this Development Guide, and your notes, on a regular basis in the future.

3

Legacy Practice 4

ADVOCATING DIFFERENCES AND COMMUNITY

Critical Success Skills: Core Competencies

Legacy Leaders acknowledge the importance and benefit of differences, and have an openness to diverse perspectives. They work hard to remove labels and prejudices, overcome comfort zones, and eliminate "rubber stamp" and "cookie cutter" mentality. Becoming a successful advocator of differences and community requires a keen desire to know others as people, not mere resources, and an understanding that when one grows and succeeds, all do. Advocating differences develops a passion for learning and discovery that unites these differences into community process instead of personal agenda. The ten critical success skills for this Legacy Practice serve to generate a team-building environment that tears down personal, departmental or organizational "walls" or silos, and fabricates a healthy culture based on understanding the community strength and ultimate success afforded in differences.

1. Be able to take a stand for a person, practice or cause.
2. Constantly raise visibility of individuals by mentoring and developing them.
3. Advocate for a strengths-based culture.
4. Be a connoisseur of talent, recognizing, valuing and utilizing the best each person has to offer.

Legacy Practice 4: **DEVELOPMENT GUIDE**

5. Insist on building teams with diverse approaches and capabilities.

6. Look for and create cross-functional opportunities to develop unique talent.

7. Promote inter-departmental collaboration, rather than "silo" orientation.

8. Consider impact of actions on greater community (beyond organization).

9. Maintain ongoing dialogue/involvement with internal/external communities.

10. Promote inclusive environment to unite toward common focus.

Consideration: Professional Development

1. Are you able to "take a stand" for what is right, and stand with those who stand for right? Are you a ready advocate? What person, situation, practice or cause exists in your life (business or otherwise) right now that you can take a stand for? Have you? How? If not, why not and what can you do about it?

2. Do you take a stand for what (or who) you believe is right in your area of responsibility? What are the risks of doing this? Are you willing to take them? What are the results?

Legacy Practice 4: DEVELOPMENT GUIDE

3. How do you know when to not stand, or to change your stand? What is your typical behavior pattern in these times?

4. Do you have the attitude, and heart desire, to mentor others?

5. Can you, at any given time, easily state the strengths of each of your team members, and say with assurance, that each one is in the right place, doing the right thing, working from their strengths?

6. What are you doing today to know and employ the strengths of your team members? Are desired outcomes the result? Do you know *your own* strengths, and are you working from those strengths? If not, how can this be corrected?

7. Describe your current team. What are your team members' individual differences? How could this team be more diverse, and how would that diversity contribute to its strength?

4

8. Do you honestly acknowledge differences and recognize the value of diversity? Do you put it to work for you? How?

Legacy Practice 4: DEVELOPMENT GUIDE

9. Some teams pride themselves on the fact that they all "think alike." If that is the case, then there are big holes in their thinking and big opportunities lost. Do all of your team members think alike? Are you all "from the same mold?" What value could be derived from diversity in thought, as well as every other area?

10. Do you have the ability to *recognize* ability? If so, what do you do with it? How do you leverage it for successful attainment of goals?

11. How have you cultivated your ability to recognize talent? Do you understand the importance of doing so? Do you *make the most of* this talent to achieve results? What opportunities exist right now in your area to practice being a connoisseur of talent?

12. Have you honestly attempted to identify skills, competencies, strengths and talents in those around you, not only within your area of responsibility, but in other areas? Can you identify at least one strength in each person you work with? How about one "budding" unique talent in each? Are these people currently working in places and on projects where those strengths and unique talents are showcased and developed? How, or why not? If not, what can you do about it?

4

Legacy Practice 4: DEVELOPMENT GUIDE

13. What are the risks to developing cross-functional talent? Do you take these risks, and if so, how do you handle them? What are the benefits?

14. What are your top three "greater community" groups within your organization? How would you describe the quality of your communication with these groups, and your level of involvement. Could it be better? How, and what will you do about it? If appropriate, do the same exercise for the top three groups/individuals *outside* the organization.

15. What kind of plan can you develop to maintain the whole system health of your organization and external communities?

16. What are you currently doing to promote an inclusive environment that unites toward common focus? What else can you do?

4

17. Are you dependent, independent or interdependent in your area of responsibility?

Legacy Practice 4: DEVELOPMENT GUIDE

Essence: *Being* a Legacy Leader
BE-Attitudes of an Advocator of Differences and Community

Great leaders who successfully apply this Legacy Practice will have a
number of attitudes, traits and characteristics which allow them to fully
advocate for differences and community. We could include such things as
partnership-oriented, non-territorial, sharing, an enabler, and a promoter.
These attitudes are all necessary. For leaders to truly live their legacy in
this practice, however, there are some foundational BE-attitudes necessary
to elevate their leadership from significance to legacy. We have listed the
features we consider the Top Five BE-attitudes for your consideration in
this Legacy Practice. These are not listed in any order of importance. Brief
descriptions follow.

A Legacy Leader, an Advocator of Differences and Community, IS:

1. **A Champion**
2. **Inclusive/Uniter**
3. **Community-Minded**
4. **Discerning**
5. **Expectant** (Sense of Expectancy)

4

1. A Champion
This person is a ready advocate for individuals, or causes. They are natural
encouragers, supporters, defenders and upholders. These leaders are others-
centered, always seeking opportunities to champion people and issues
worthy of support. These people are, however, careful and thoughtful in
this support, taking a stand only after discerning whether or not people or
issues align with their values.

2. Inclusive/A Uniter

This person has a natural or practiced ability to unite people in teams, for causes, to achieve results and to develop community. This inclusiveness always seeks uniquenesses and strengths to add to the overall vigor of the community, and has the ability to recognize value in diversity where others may not.

3. Community-Minded

This person is able to identify common denominators and uniting factors in groups, and uses these commonalities to build teams of people with shared goals. These leaders understand that the greatest accomplishments are the result of working together as a whole, where every individual is valued and recognized.

4. Discerning

This person has either an inherent or cultivated ability to make solid decisions and judgments based on sound consideration of all information available. He or she is able to distinguish between close and seemingly similar things for the betterment of self and others. These leaders are able to determine and recognize individual gifts, strengths and uniquenesses. This ability allows them to build strong diverse teams.

4

5. Expectant (Sense of Expectancy)

This person is always expecting results, anticipating goals to be met and people to work together to achieve common objectives. This expectancy is modeled to others who then sense, understand and therefore work toward stated goals, often with a renewed focus or urgency. These leaders have a clear sense of vision, strategies and ultimate purpose for being in community, on which their expectancy is based.

Legacy Practice 4: DEVELOPMENT GUIDE

BE-ATTITUDE SELF ASSESSMENT

How developed is your core being for becoming a Legacy Leader in this Legacy Practice? After reading the descriptions of these BE-Attitudes above, rate yourself *(circle one)* on the following scale, then go on to the steps and questions that follow.

BE-ATTITUDES of an Advocator of Differences and Community		RATING: 5=all the time, 0=not at all					
1	I am a champion for others.	5	4	3	2	1	0
2	I am inclusive, a uniter.	5	4	3	2	1	0
3	I am community-minded.	5	4	3	2	1	0
4	I am discerning.	5	4	3	2	1	0
5	I have a sense of expectancy.	5	4	3	2	1	0

Where do your ratings fall? How many 5's? Any 2's or below? Any zeros? Here are some suggestions for building the core being of an Advocator of Differences and Community.

1. ***Choose your two highest ratings.*** Determine how you can leverage these strengths to be even more effective in developing and living your leadership legacy. ***Also choose two of your lowest*** rating attitudes to be your "work on" areas for improvement. Use the questions below to build your BE-attitudes.

2. ***Think of someone you know to be this***, to have this attitude, for each of the two areas you selected for improvement. For example, if you scored yourself low in being seamless in your behavior in all places, who do you know whose behavior *is* seamless (past or present)? Identify one person for each of the areas you want to develop and do the following exercises. Write the attitudes and person's name in the space provided:

4

Legacy Practice 4: DEVELOPMENT GUIDE

ATTITUDE   **PERSON I KNOW WHO DISPLAYS THIS ATTITUDE**

1.

2.

Consider the following for each attitude, and person listed:

a. What does this person do that lets me, and others, know he or she is
    _____ (BE-Attitude)?

b. How can I emulate this behavior/attitude?

c. How will this behavior help me become a better leader? A Legacy
    Leader?

3. After completing the above steps, **make a commitment** to improve.
    Choose one of your "work on" attitudes each week, and focus on
    improving that attitude in all you think, do and speak.

    a. Be aware of your behavior and thought processes during the week, as
        they pertain to that attitude.

    b. Create a mental reminder that will alert you to old behavior and
        thought patterns you want to change.

    c. When you are alerted to old behavior and thought patterns, change
        them immediately, if possible. If not, use that experience to help
        remind you in the future. Consider what triggered this old behavior
        or attitude, and how you can respond differently in the future.

4

      d. Evaluate your week for progress and determine how you can improve this attitude next week.

      e. The following week, add another "work on" attitude as your focus, without neglecting the first one.

      f. Keep doing this until you notice a definite change (improvement), so that your improved attitude has become part of you, part of your core being as a Legacy Leader. Chances are if *you* notice an improvement, others will as well.

      g. If journaling is familiar and comfortable for you, consider keeping track of your BE-Attitude development. Brush away discouragement if things don't change immediately. They will, especially if this is the way you want to be. Sometimes we just need to rethink or reframe how we think and do.

Application: Putting it to Work

Are you ready to *be* an advocator, not just *do* advocating? The "Legacy Steps" on the next page can place you firmly on the stairway. However, before committing yourself to climbing these stairs, look long and hard at the first steps in both advocating differences, and advocating community. *Set aside your ego, and choose to be inclusive.* Are you sure you're ready? These are fundamental choices that every great leader makes, and then resolves to live and lead by. Can you do it?

Legacy Practice 4: DEVELOPMENT GUIDE

Legacy Steps to Advocating DIFFERENCES

1. Set aside your ego.

2. Discover and actively work to overcome your personal biases, prejudices and stereotypes.

3. Actively seek out differences and the strengths within them.

4. Look for common ground where you previously saw only islands of difference.

5. Reframe how you think and approach people that are "different." Take time and make the effort to understand others.

6. Become an active and eager listener.

7. Actively seek out the opinions of those who may think differently, and value them.

8. Design conversations and meetings to be inclusive, then recap for understanding.

9. Remember that you don't have all the answers and other perspectives can provide valuable insight.

10. Discard old ideas of territorialism and self-protection, work to lift up others, and understand that many parts make a whole.

4

Legacy Practice 4: DEVELOPMENT GUIDE

Legacy Steps to Advocating COMMUNITY

1. Choose to be inclusive.

2. Open doors, take down walls, and break through any barriers between you and others.

3. Seek every opportunity to acknowledge and respect the contributions of others.

4. Help others discover their strengths, and potential contribution to the whole.

5. Evaluate your existing communication protocols and habits, then work to widen the circle and increase the frequency and informative content.

6. Practice sharing information with those outside perceived departmental or team boundaries.

7. Discover your own unique strengths and perspectives.

8. Remind yourself that you are serving the vision of the whole organization, and that involves every individual, every team, and every department.

9. Support and defend the community as a whole, and bring to light activities and behaviors that do not have this effect.

10. Be a leader who enables rather than hobbles the growth and inclusion of all people within the whole organizational community.

Legacy Shifts: Expected Outcomes

We learned in grade school that kick-ball, hide-and-seek, and baseball, among other things, don't usually work well when we play by ourselves. We also quickly applied the concept that a baseball team composed solely of shortstops and catchers won't win many games. A pitching ace, outfielders with great throwing arms, and some power hitters were generally the first among our picks for teammates. Somewhere along the line, however, we seem to have misplaced these life lessons and forgotten that those dynamics apply also to business pursuits. When Legacy Leaders advocate for differences and community unity in the organization, they realize more "wins" and celebrate more successes—together. The success skills for this Legacy Practice are the business team's "dugout rules" and when they are consistently practiced, the team experiences amazing transformations. Individual players become team winners.

FROM "us against them"...**TO esprit de corps**
Instead of inter-departmental/positional and territorial posturing and exclusion, an attitude of "we're all in this together" is promoted and celebrated. Every position, every department, every person is acknowledged and encouraged for their valuable contribution to the whole.

FROM "he doesn't have a clue"... **TO "what can he share?"**
Instead of snap labels, personal prejudices and excluding biases that shut down communication and contribution, an actively encouraged attitude of inclusion opens doors to new perspectives, unique possibilities, and greater potential.

4

Legacy Practice 4: **DEVELOPMENT GUIDE**

FROM Individuals...**TO Relationships**

Individuals working individually cannot accomplish nearly what individuals working in relationship can achieve. When an attitude of openly accepting differences is promoted, a unique connectivity is the result, one which energizes and advances both the individual and the relationship—and the organizational vision.

FROM exclusion...**TO inclusion**

Instead of excluding the thoughts, ideas, strengths and perspectives of individuals outside perceived boundaries, the Legacy Leader actively seeks to include as many as possible, wherever possible and appropriate, in the community of the whole.

FROM the "darkness beyond"...**TO enlightened communication**

Instead of leaving others "in the dark" from a lack of inclusive communication, leaders are deliberate about bringing the whole into a complete communication loop, keeping all informed and up to date. Good and thoughtful communication is an important element of showing respect and acknowledging the potential contribution of others.

FROM scattered pieces...**TO a healthy whole**

Instead of many pieces functioning independently, and often without the benefit of input or feedback from "outside" pieces, the organization functions smoothly as an entity, with all pieces contributing to the successful operation of the whole.

4

Legacy Practice 4: DEVELOPMENT GUIDE

NOTES

Use this space to jot down any thoughts you might have about your legacy development. Consider referencing this Development Guide, and your notes, on a regular basis in the future.

4

Legacy Practice 5

CALIBRATING RESPONSIBILITY AND ACCOUNTABILITY

Critical Success Skills: Core Competencies

A calibrator consistently compares results against vision and values, and to established milestones and road maps. He or she provides a good and consistent example of accomplishing tasks and meeting shared goals, seeks to determine if actions measure up to standards and levels of excellence, and shows where learning is needed and new behaviors need to be developed. This leader keeps both internal and external focus, is ready and able to observe and respond to change and equips and congratulates everyone for responsible, professional efforts. This kind of calibration of responsibility and accountability is not about discipline, punishment, hall monitors, rule books or pointed fingers. It is a standard set by leadership by which the whole community has ownership of the process—and therefore is wholly accountable for progress made during that process. These critical success skills outline the behaviors that enable the leader to guide all individual parts of the community to contribute their very best to the process and share the results.

1. Execute the organization's strategic plan and use appropriate checks and balances to reach the goals.

2. Have your "finger on the pulse" of the organization and know your milestone status.

3. Be sure individuals on your team are clear about position responsibilities and how they fit into the organization's direction and deliverables.

5

Legacy Practice 5: **DEVELOPMENT GUIDE**

4. Require peak performance and support everyone with appropriate resources.

5. Provide regular feedback and coaching, and take action when performance does not meet stated expectations.

6. Have clearly defined accountabilities for yourself and for your organization.

7. Have a clearly developed action plan with benchmarks and milestones, and provisions for making adjustments along the way.

8. Model a sense of urgency both in getting things done and responding to change.

9. Be alert to trends that potentially affect results, and re-calibrate action plans where necessary.

10. Gain commitment from everyone in your area of responsibility, and have established accountabilities with appropriate consequences and rewards.

Consideration: Professional Development

1. What thoughts do you have on a personal level about accountability? Are there any areas of your professional or personal life where accountability, or responsibility, needs to be defined and reinforced? What can you do about those?

2. What plan do you have in place to make corrections and adjustments if you have discovered that you are not in alignment with your stated performance indicators?

Legacy Practice 5:   DEVELOPMENT GUIDE

3.   How aware are you of course and direction? How frequently do you check the mile markers? How do you know when you need to make adjustments? How will you implement alignments back to stated strategy? How will you lead your team members to follow and make their own adjustments?

4.   How would you rate your ability to determine the need to make adjustments to strategies and action plans? How could you improve this ability?

5.   How would you define "checks and balances" within an organization? What should it look like? How should it function? How does this apply to you and your area of responsibility within your organization?

6.   How, and how often, do you consciously "take the pulse" of your organization, and your area of responsibility? Has it become so automatic that you always have your "finger on the pulse?" Do you know at any given time the "health" of your organization, or your team? If not, what can you do now in order to never lose that focus?

5

Legacy Practice 5: **DEVELOPMENT GUIDE**

7. Whose responsibility is it to make sure people know they matter to the organization's direction and deliverables? Do your team members know their mission, their value, and their fit in the organization? How is this periodically revisited and monitored? How does this relate to your area of responsibility, and what are you doing, or can you do, about it?

8. Have you gained commitment from everyone in your area of responsibility? How do you know? How is it demonstrated? How is it earned?

9. Are your team members convinced of your integrity? Do they trust you? Do they know you speak the truth, and have authority? How? How do you make a conscious call for commitment?

10. Do you have a plan for consequences and rewards? Have you given this ample thought before you need to implement either of these accountability factors? Do your team members know them? Are they committed to their follow-through? Are *you* committed to this follow-through?

5

11. Exactly how do you require peak performance? How do you communicate your requirement for this, and how do you hold people accountable for it? What do you do when performance expectations are not met?

12. Do you provide regular feedback and coaching for those in your area of responsibility? How? How would you describe your style in this? Have you acted as coach when giving feedback? How do people respond? Consider your current style. How could you improve in this area?

13. Describe your typical action steps when confronted with performance that does not meet stated standards. Consider your personal performance in these times, and that of others, either individually or corporately. What is your attitude? How do you coach through these times?

14. Do you have personal accountabilities? What are they, and how do you hold yourself accountable for them? Do your personal accountabilities show self-awareness?

15. Legacy Leaders hold themselves accountable for excellence above expectation. How can you cultivate this attitude in yourself, and in your team members? What would be the result if everyone worked this way?

5

Legacy Practice 5: **DEVELOPMENT GUIDE**

16. How alert are you to trends that potentially affect results? What tools do you use to do this? What is your priority and attitude about this? What trends, in particular, are of primary interest to you in your area of responsibility, and how do you remain alert to them?

17. How can you be pro-active in your re-calibration of action plans for your area of responsibility?

18. How, exactly, do you model urgency for your team members? How do you do this without forfeiting needed pauses, and without creating a "frantic" environment? Define your sense of urgency in getting things done, and meeting the organization's vision and goals.

19. How aware are you of the need for change and the urgency involved in making those changes? What cautions could be applied here?

20. How well do you respond to change, and to the need for change? How do you help your team members do this? How do you teach others to be flexible and agile in their response to change and chaos?

5

Legacy Practice 5: DEVELOPMENT GUIDE

Essence: *Being* a Legacy Leader
BE-Attitudes of a Calibrator of Responsibility and Accountability

We would expect the core being, the essence of a Calibrator of Responsibility and Accountability, to include such BE-attitudes as responsible, consistent, accountable, vision-grounded, and a problem solver to begin the list. As we have stated before, however, a *Legacy* Leader's BE-attitudes and aptitudes begin with a foundational core that all other attitudes and qualities will build upon or derive from. These core essentials are what allow the great leader to build leadership legacy, and apply learning to become true Calibrators of Responsibility and Accountability. We have listed the features we consider the Top Five BE-attitudes for your consideration in this Legacy Practice. These are not listed in any order of importance. Brief descriptions follow.

A Legacy Leader, a Calibrator of Responsibility and Accountability, IS:

1. **Results-Oriented**
2. **An Analyst**
3. **Vigilant/Committed**
4. **Aware/Alert**
5. **Answerable**

1. Results-Oriented
This person has a definite clarity of purpose and uses this clarity to drive behavior and performance to achieve results. These leaders have complete understanding of *why* they and others do *anything*, and always align their actions toward accomplishing goals and meeting vision. They never take their eye off desired results. There is very little to no "wasted motion" for these people. They tend to take advantage of every opportunity to produce results.

5

Legacy Practice 5: **DEVELOPMENT GUIDE**

2. **An Analyst**

This person has the ability to analyze, diagnose and evaluate information, situations, issues or the environment around them. This is generally an inherent trait, but can be developed with focused practice. These people are usually able to "take in" details and information automatically in a way that allows them to constantly be aware of the real picture, wherever they are, whatever they are doing. They notice things that others may miss, and generally use the information to maintain a truthful picture of situations and conditions.

3. **Vigilant/Committed**

This person is constantly attentive and observant and able to "size up" things quickly. These people tend to be watchful at all times. This aptitude goes hand in hand with the one above, the ability to analyze. As the vigilant person takes in data, that data is analyzed automatically to yield accurate feedback on any situation at any time. Vigilant leaders are also committed to their vision and stated goals, and to their vigilance in keeping them.

4. **Aware/Alert**

This person has either an inherent or practiced awareness of the world around them. These leaders are able, at any given time, to provide an accurate and truthful portrait of their environments. They are not only aware of details and whole pictures, but are also alert to potential changes. They generally have internal "markers" set as guidelines for analysis and comparison. Again, this attitude is a refinement of the ones above. An analyst must be able to take the information in, be alert, aware and vigilant in this data gathering process, in order to accurately diagnose and evaluate.

5

5. Answerable

This person innately understands and practices responsibility and accountability. They hold themselves answerable to others to perform, and then liable to account for that performance. These leaders have complete awareness of the concept of action and reaction, behavior and consequences. They are guided by internal values and will model behavior that influences others to do the same. These people have no understanding of "ducking blame," don't engage in cover ups, and are completely open to scrutiny.

BE-ATTITUDE SELF ASSESSMENT

How developed is your core being for becoming a Legacy Leader in this Legacy Practice? After reading the descriptions of these BE-Attitudes above, rate yourself *(circle one)* on the following scale, then go on to the steps and questions that follow.

BE-ATTITUDES of a Calibrator of Responsibility and Accountability		RATING: 5=all the time, 0=not at all					
1	I am results-oriented.	5	4	3	2	1	0
2	I am an analyst.	5	4	3	2	1	0
3	I am vigilant and committed.	5	4	3	2	1	0
4	I am aware and alert.	5	4	3	2	1	0
5	I am answerable.	5	4	3	2	1	0

Where do your ratings fall? How many 5's? Any 2's or below? Any zeros? Here are some suggestions for building the core being of a Calibrator of Responsibility and Accountability.

1. ***Choose your two highest ratings.*** Determine how you can leverage these strengths to be even more effective in developing and living your

5

Legacy Practice 5: DEVELOPMENT GUIDE

leadership legacy. ***Also choose two of your lowest*** rating attitudes to be your "work on" areas for improvement. Use the questions below to build your BE-attitudes.

2. ***Think of someone you know to be this***, to have this attitude, for each of the two areas you selected for improvement. For example, if you scored yourself low in being seamless in your behavior in all places, who do you know whose behavior *is* seamless (past or present)? Identify one person for each of the areas you want to develop and do the following exercises. Write the attitudes and person's name in the space provided:

   ATTITUDE   **PERSON I KNOW WHO DISPLAYS THIS ATTITUDE**

   1.

   2.

   Consider the following for each attitude, and person listed:

   a. What does this person do that lets me, and others, know he or she is
   _____ (BE-Attitude)?

   b. How can I emulate this behavior/attitude?

   c. How will this behavior help me become a better leader? A Legacy Leader?

3. After completing the above steps, ***make a commitment*** to improve. Choose one of your "work on" attitudes each week, and focus on improving that attitude in all you think, do and speak.

5

Legacy Practice 5: DEVELOPMENT GUIDE

a. Be aware of your behavior and thought processes during the week, as they pertain to that attitude.

b. Create a mental reminder that will alert you to old behavior and thought patterns you want to change.

c. When you are alerted to old behavior and thought patterns, change them immediately, if possible. If not, use that experience to help remind you in the future. Consider what triggered this old behavior or attitude, and how you can respond differently in the future.

d. Evaluate your week for progress and determine how you can improve this attitude next week.

e. The following week, add another "work on" attitude as your focus, but don't forget or neglect the first one.

f. Keep doing this until you notice a definite change (improvement), so that your improved attitude has become part of you, part of your core being as a Legacy Leader. Chances are if *you* notice an improvement, others will as well.

g. If journaling is familiar and comfortable for you, consider keeping track of your BE-Attitude development. Brush away discouragement if things don't change immediately. They will, especially if this is the way you want to be. Sometimes we just need to rethink or reframe how we think and do.

5

Legacy Practice 5: **DEVELOPMENT GUIDE**

Application: Putting it all Together

Calibrating responsibility and accountability should not be an uphill battle against the native tendencies toward blame, blissful ignorance, or denial. It will require diligence, but committed leadership can make this practice natural and comfortable—and routine. Are you ready to remove your head from the sand and soar? These "Legacy Steps" on the next page will provide a path to the launching pad. As with all leadership competencies this practice requires your *choice* to *be* a *Legacy* Leader, not just *do* leadership.

Legacy Steps to Calibrating **RESPONSIBILITY**

1. Be responsible, and expect the same of everyone else.

2. Observe and optimize employee performance by ensuring the right people are in the right positions.

3. Acknowledge all contributions and celebrate all successes.

4. Maintain a vigilant, ongoing comparison of all behaviors to vision and values.

5. Inspire acceptable standards of behavior in others by providing the right role model.

6. Establish road maps and targeted milestones for measurement of progress toward vision.

7. Dwell on the present and the future, not the past.

5

8. Make all perceived "failures" into opportunities and challenges.

9. Make appropriate adjustments to new information and changes.

10. Be sure all expectations and standards for acceptable behavior are clearly communicated, both through role modeling and other understandable means.

11. Make no exceptions.

Legacy Steps to Calibrating ACCOUNTABILITY

1. Hold yourself accountable at all times.

2. Set and communicate clear standards.

3. Communicate community accountability—no exceptions.

4. Remind others that the highest goal of accountability is to satisfy the customer, the vendor or other target of organizational vision.

5. Encourage frequent personal accountability checks.

6. Perform regular community process accountability sessions to evaluate the process and outcomes.

7. Encourage frequent and clear communication among all parts of the whole.

8. Encourage relationship building among employees, but not "cliques."

5

Legacy Practice 5: DEVELOPMENT GUIDE

9. Understand the differences between short-term and long-term performance outcomes, and be sure your understanding is communicated well.

10. Work to keep the community of workers in partnership and ownership of the overall process and fully able and willing to be accountable.

Legacy Shifts: Expected Outcomes

We may have a natural propensity for blame and finger pointing, but we can choose to outgrow this inclination. Blame only creates a circle of confusion and distraction, and ultimately paralysis. Responsibility and accountability can unfold the circle into a straight line of forward progress. By practicing the calibrating of responsibility and accountability, we can cause shifts from distraction to determination, and encourage thinking about how to meet goals and overcome challenges through acceptable behaviors. What went wrong is in the past, and serves no purpose other than learning. What went right adds insight, energy and value to the community. When a winning football team suffers an unexpected and humiliating loss in front of millions of Monday Night Football viewers, they can't afford the luxury of blame. Early Tuesday morning this team drags out the films and memorizes every play and every move, analyzing for improvement. Each player is responsible for shifts in play, so that together they can create constructive accountability that will lead to a victory celebration the next time they take the field.

5

Legacy Practice 5: DEVELOPMENT GUIDE

FROM what went wrong...**TO how can we do it better?**
Instead of focusing on the "mistakes" or failed behavior, a shift to focusing
on what went right, then to how something can be accomplished in a more
responsible manner, allows for constructive learning and growth.

FROM do your own thing...**TO doing the responsible thing**
Instead of a wide range of varying degrees of responsibility and behaviors
concerning a targeted goal, calibrated responsibility gives everyone a clear
picture of what is expected, and how to perform responsibly, beginning
with—and modeled by—the leader.

FROM mismatched...**TO perfect match**
Instead of employees whose strengths and skills do not match
their position, the organization practicing the calibration of responsibility
actively seeks to place people in the positions where they can make the
greatest contribution, use all the strengths they have developed,
and grow the ones with potential. This calibration effort
involves ongoing observation for optimization of employee skills.

FROM worker...**TO owner**
Instead of working as a "paid employee" to do a job for someone else, the
worker becomes an owner in the accountability process,
sharing all challenges and giving his or her best to the process.
Some companies have chosen to actually make their employees
owners from a financial standpoint, but even without this arrangement
leaders can make intellectual and emotional owners of every individual,
inviting their freely given best for the benefit of the whole.

5

Legacy Practice 5: *DEVELOPMENT GUIDE*

FROM "it's on YOUR head..." **TO it's on OUR shoulders**

Instead of looking for scapegoats and "blamees" for failed process or outcome, the Legacy Leader can create a shift to shared accountability, and shared process for achievement and success. "Who did what wrong" is not so important as "How can we do it better?" The shoulders of accountability are wide and collective, not individual.

FROM doing my job...**TO celebrating our achievement**

Instead of a lot of individuals just "doing their jobs," the community whole shares in the accountability as well as the celebration of process and outcome. Growth occurs on an individual as well as a community level when each part is accountable to the whole. Community accountability ensures shared participation in both challenges and victories.

5

NOTES

Use this space to jot down any thoughts you might have about your legacy development. Consider referencing this Development Guide, and your notes, on a regular basis in the future.

5

Appendix

TWO

Using The
Legacy Leadership
Model

Legacy Leadership is a complete framework for building great leadership, both in individuals and whole organizations. We'd like to offer a few suggestions for effective application of this model.

Seasoned Leaders

Even if you have "been around the block" in the leadership theater and your orchestra is accomplished, you can still use a little calibration, some fine-tuning, to make your leadership even better, and your effectiveness and influence even wider. Chances are that by now you already know that these critical success skills are indeed what make leadership work. But are they what make *your* leadership work? Set aside your ego a bit and open the door to the possibility that even you can improve. You may wish to pursue self-development on your own, or consider engaging an experienced executive coach familiar with Legacy Leadership. A good coach can often enable you to reach higher levels of leadership excellence than you would on your own. These coaches can partner with you and become the multiplication factor for more timely results. In this ever-expanding information age, leaders often need a competitive edge. That edge may be your executive coach. Either way, remember that all of us can refresh our understanding and measurement of great leadership on a regular basis. You never graduate as a leader. Continue being a life-long student of leadership.

Emerging Leaders

For all of you fresh faces just beginning your leadership journey, you can't have a better guidebook to *great* leadership than Legacy Leadership. This model provides a comprehensive yet flexible and adaptable framework on which to build your own leadership greatness. Study it, know it, apply it and *be* it whenever and wherever you can. Determine where you are now and decide where you want to be. In some ways, you have the advantage of beginning the path to greatness now, at this early stage of your leadership, over those who have gone before you without the benefit of this platform for success. You have in your hands what works, and what does not. And as you flex your muscles during leadership workouts, you will gain valuable conditioning and perspective if you keep these tenets before you. Choose now to be a life-long student of leadership. Keep learning, keep *desiring* to learn and grow, and keep holding your vision of being a great leader—a *Legacy* Leader. Seek, and invite, mentors who model these leadership practices—and become a mentor yourself. No matter where you are now in leadership prowess, there is always

> Keep learning, keep *desiring* to learn and grow, and keep holding your vision of being a great leader... a *Legacy* Leader.

someone else who can benefit from *your* experience and knowledge. Align yourself with organizations and other people who exhibit *legacy* leadership competencies and attitudes. Be committed to the process of *being* a great leader. Emerging leaders can also consider partnering with experienced executive coaches who can radically advance this process.

Organizations

Most companies today provide some kind of leadership development and training for their employees. Most often, however, it consists of individual components that usually are not linked together by an integrated structure and complete framework. Whether this training and development is conducted internally, or externally facilitated, Legacy Leadership can provide the means to achieve an organization-wide leadership culture. It is a way to bring everyone onto the same page, all working with the same internal compass. It can be the stage on which an entire organization becomes great, not just individual leaders and employees. Organizations that promote standardized leadership models are promoting standardized behaviors and competencies, which all promote healthier bottom lines. And the more complete the model, the more complete the transformation. Organizations can consider bringing in executive coaches and professional trainers, or choose to undertake both coaching and training internally, using Legacy Leadership as the organizational manual to achieve success— individually and corporately. Legacy Leadership is applicable at every organizational level, from the shipping docks to the penthouse boardroom. It is adaptable to any industry, any work place.

Coaches, Consultants and Others

In the preface of this book we told you how Legacy Leadership came to be. We are experienced executive coaches, and we authored this leadership system originally in order to have a complete model to coach against, something to measure progress and assist in constructing a targeted yet comprehensive development plan. If you are an executive coach, Legacy Leadership can be the long-missing model that provides a well-rounded, scalable leadership platform on which to base your coaching. Even when individuals or organizations have a leadership model in place, Legacy Leadership can be the foundational platform on which others reside. It plugs all the holes and gives a structure to support other techniques. Just about every other leadership model will find a place to live inside Legacy Leadership. And for those clients who have no existing model, Legacy Leadership will provide the kind of model to achieve well-rounded leadership competency. It will assist the coach in measuring current levels of leadership, as well as planning for the development of future greatness, without any missing pieces. This model allows you to work on individual competencies or whole practice areas. It addresses both the being and the doing of a leader, and can become a vital tool for executive coaches who wish to fully develop clients, not just address single issues. *(CoachWorks International also offers both self and complete 360 feedback online assessment services in Legacy Leadership, with multiple customization options. Visit the website at www.coachworks.com for more information.)* We encourage you to investigate how this model can provide the train tracks for long distance travel in developing client leadership excellence, and grow yourself as well.

Hold the vision and values of what you want to become,
create opportunities to be that kind of leader,
influence yourself in ways that promote this attitude,
advocate this kind of leadership in yourself, and
calibrate it—until you become it.

CoachWorks® International, Inc. was founded in 1995 by Dr. Jeannine Sandstrom and Dr. Lee Smith, executive leader coaches who developed the Legacy Leadership model. Drs. Sandstrom and Smith are highly experienced executive leader coaches who facilitate sustainable results in the areas of critical and current concern for top-level clients. After years of industry experience, CoachWorks International has a proven record in leadership development and helping clients realize solutions to the top issues concerning executives today. Lee and Jeannine partner with executives to optimize leadership performance. Their passion and success are focused in working with leaders who want to accelerate their strategic effectiveness and sustain organizational vitality. This work is delivered via individual leader coaching at the board, officer and leadership team level; facilitating leader team learning and planning sessions; and delivering Legacy Leadership Institutes designed by CoachWorks for emerging and seasoned leaders. Both authors work with leaders, executives, independent contributors, entrepreneurs and leadership teams as they deal with performance and competitive challenges. They identify and build on existing competencies to create a bridge toward desired personal and professional outcomes and corporate strategic goals.

Smith and Sandstrom are passionate about optimizing leadership performance in the individual leader as well as his or her team using the most technologically advanced whole systems interaction tools. As pioneers in the coaching profession, Lee and Jeannine use an innovative process developed specifically to assist professionals, business leaders, CEOs and their organizations to achieve goals. As Executive Team Coaches they use a consultative coach approach to having teams raise their standards of innovative collaboration. CoachWorks' mission is to be a partner with leaders who want to transform their leadership abilities to bridge the gap between professional achievement, personal significance...and legacy. The Legacy Leadership model was developed to provide a foundation and framework for this professional development, and has been tested and proven for ten years with individuals and whole organizations.

Dr. Sandstrom and Dr. Smith are founding board members of Corporate Coach U, an international corporate and executive coach training firm with graduates worldwide, delivering valued executive and corporate coaching based on curriculum, models and codified experience. Lee and Jeannine co-authored these extensive training courses for CCU. They have also authored numerous books and coaching programs, including the Professional Foundations for Masterful Coaches, the Coaching Clinic for Managers and Leaders©, the Personal Coaching Styles Inventory (PCSI)©, and the Executive's Professional Foundations Program©, and have assisted in establishing the standards, ethics and principles of the coaching profession. Jeannine and Lee co-convened an Executive Coach Summit for the International Coach Federation (ICF) to distinguish the profession of Executive Coaching, and also write for professional journals and white papers for ICF. Both participate regularly at national and international professional conferences as showcased speakers.

We work with leaders who are already successful. We partner with them to sustain growth and continued achievement. In today's world of unprecedented change and speed of growth, executives know that what got them there won't keep them there. They have to keep growing and stretching to meet new competitive demands. Our clients are highly valued and known for their technical and operational abilities, even their leadership skills, yet they have a sense that there is more to life than just the business game, and we help them discover greater vistas of opportunity. Much of our work is at the officer level. We also partner with junior leadership and management individuals and teams, as well as entire boards of directors. Our clients:

- **are already highly successful,** looking for their "next edge"
- **are already working on something big,** or want to work on something big, something they are passionate about (they are "up to something" in their lives)
- **value an external resource** for challenging status quo, empowerment, accountability, safety, etc.
- **are fun to work with** (excited about growth and discovery)

We bring a blend of services to our clients, whom we believe all deserve our very best. We advise, consult, teach, coach, support, question and challenge. We partner for performance enhancement, effective leadership and mentoring, and sustainable and measurable results. We act as a catalyst for clarity and sustainable focus, and hold leaders accountable for change.

We help leaders stand out from the rest.

Our clients say...

- Since there is no school for CEOs, coaching is an intense private executive education experience.

- They are specialists in the technology of human interaction.

- They helped us understand why people don't do what they want to do, and get beyond that point to actually doing what we wanted to do.

- They have a capacity for helping people see blind spots, and do things differently to get better results.

- ...our secret weapon for growth and change.

- ...a place to be heard, where I'm safe. I can try new things. I know someone cares, will tell me the truth without any agenda. I don't have that anywhere else.

- I wanted to really look at my influence, my impact for legacy, in both my personal life and my business results. My coach helped see much farther than I could on my own.

- ...a time out that keeps me on track in my busy world.

- Helped me work through the complexities of leading a growing organization.

- CEOs operate in isolation...my coaching is the only place where I felt truly heard and understood.

- There was no manipulation, no expectation about who I should be or how I should act. It was really freeing, and productive. I rediscovered my visions and dreams and I am excited and prepared to fulfill them now.

- ...my private "board of director" to keep me accountable.

- I learned I can't do it all, yet my people can when I'm focused on their development.

Contact us to go farther on your professional journey.

CoachWorks International, Inc.

Dr. Jeannine Sandstrom

Prior to CoachWorks, Jeannine launched and led three national management development consultancies focusing on leadership emergencies, strategic plan implementation for merger and acquisition and emerging leader team development.

Dr. Sandstrom has also coached executive leaders at The Prudential, Fidelity Investments, Chase Bank, John Deere, NASA, Puget Sound Energy, ARCO, private brokerage organizations, Merrill Lynch, Oracle, Samson Resources and numerous entrepreneurial and not-for-profit organizations. She has participated in Public Broadcasting Service (PBS) presentations, and has had featured articles in the *Professional Mentor and Coach Journal*, as well as *The Wall Street Journal* and *Fortune Magazine*. She is a founding contributor to the International Consortium for Coaching in Organizations; a founding editorial board member of the International Journal of Coaching in Organizations, has served on the (Dallas, TX) Mayor's Task Force for International Development and on the boards of national professional and industry organizations, is an alumnus of LEADERSHIP DALLAS, past president of the D/FW Chapter of International Association of Career Management Professionals, a charter member of the North Texas Chapter of the international Coach Federation, and a former International Rotarian. Dr. Sandstrom holds certifications as Master Certified Coach (MCC, ICF), and Professional in Human Resources. Her doctorate is in Human Resource Development, with masters degrees in Business Administration and Adult Learning. Jeannine makes her home near Dallas, Texas.

Dr. Lee Smith

Lee worked many years with Sun Oil Company in human resources and maintained a private consultancy. As an experienced Executive Leader Coach specializing in executive leadership development and performance, Smith's clients are leaders from companies such as Tricon, IBM, Northern Telecom, Ford Motor Company, Levi Strauss, American Airlines, Baxter Healthcare, Oracle, Puget Sound Energy, Sabey Corporation, CVS/Caremark, Grant Thornton, Fidelity Investments and Samson Oil. Lee has served as an adjunct Professor and guest lecturer at the University of Texas at Dallas Executive MBA Program, University of North Texas and Abilene Christian University. She has been featured in *Newsweek*, *PBS Specials*, the *Dallas Morning News* and local television news. She has been a member of various boards including the Advisory Board of the University of North Texas, the board of Corporate Coach U and the Board of Directors of CoachInc.com. Smith frequently writes for business periodicals such as *Strategy & Business* and *Washington CEO* magazine. She has hosted the Neuroscience of Coaching Summit, and continues to mentor and develop other executive coaches to grow and distinguish the profession. Dr. Smith holds one of the first international certifications as Master Certified Coach (MCC, ICF). Smith's doctorate is in Organizational Behavior and Psychology, with an undergraduate degree in Business. Lee is a native Texan now happily transplanted in Seattle, Washington.

Appendix

FOUR

Acknowledgements

This part of the book is perhaps the most challenging to write. There are so many people who have contributed to the final product that it is difficult to know where to begin. We would be remiss unless we initially thanked and acknowledged the literally hundreds of leaders who have become the heart and soul of Legacy Leadership. Over the years of development, testing and retesting, these people have contributed valuable input and inspiration while gaining leadership competency from this model. And sincere thanks to the countless numbers of those who kept us heading in this direction by their constant inquiries about this book. We can't tell you how many times we've heard "So when are you going to get your book out?" Thank you for keeping the fires lit!

It is even more of a challenge to list the names of the many we wish to specially acknowledge and thank. There's always the fear of leaving someone out, overlooking or forgetting special people with special contributions. We are grateful to each and every one of you, mentioned or not. Please know that if our memories are failing, our hearts are not.

We want to give our very special thanks to our editor and graphic designer, Kathy Heywood. Not only has she been our constant encourager, our most helpful critic and coach, but also a stabilizer for the full development of Legacy Leadership through the years. Kathy has the wonderful ability to grasp concepts, organize thoughts and have the model come alive on the written page. Thank you for your huge contribution to Legacy Leadership.

To our Legacy Leadership training facilitators, thanks for your review and suggestions as you imparted the model to others. Thank you specifically to Jane Creswell, Carollyne Conlinn, Brenda Chaddock, Ed Allen, Dr. Kathy Dale, Mark Cappellino, Teri McEachern and Lynn Bennett, to name a few. Thanks too, to the 39 executive coach participants of the pilot teleforum as well as those attending international conferences who practiced with the model and shared it with others.

We would like to thank Jan King, our Book Publishing Strategist, who kept us focused on the right track. Also, many thanks to Steve Straus, our first coach who introduced us at the beginning of our coaching career transitions and continues to provide input into our work.

To the thousands of practicing Legacy Leaders out there, thanks for desiring to practice the art of Legacy Leadership both in your organizations and in your personal lives. And of course, to our families, whose constant support, encouragement and love has sustained us, tolerated us, and inspired us.

Finally, our heartfelt acknowledgement and thanks for the divine inspiration and enduring applicability of this model.

To all of you, please know that we are truly blessed by your collaboration and contributions, both now and into the future.

Jeannine and Lee

Index

J

Jefferson, Thomas, 70

K

Kelleher, Herb, 35, 36
Kennedy, John F., 51
King, Larry, 68

L

Lao Tzu, 114
leadership (general), xii, 25, 26 91, 92, 199
leadership "dance", 187,
leadership "music", 184
legacy (general), 19-20
    language of, 20
    living your, 19, 21, 23, 36, 46, 185, 206, 254
Legacy Leader(s), xiii, 20, 24, 192, 199, 201, 206, 222, 238, 254, 271
Legacy Leadership (general), 23-26
Legacy Living, 185-186
Legacy Practices, 26, 25-28 *(see specific practices)*
Legacy Shifts *(see expected outcomes)*
Legacy Steps *(see application)*
Lincoln, Abraham, 126
listening, 67-69, 219, 223, 224, 259
Listening Scale, 69

M

Mary Kay® Cosmetics, 94
measuring vision, 44-45
mentally agile, 223
mentor, mentoring, 128-130, 134, 240, 249, 251
mentoring chart, 130
milestones, 37, 44-45, 156, 159, 162, 203, 213, 265, 266, 267, 276
motivation, 93, 191-193, 243, 244, 246
musicians (analogy), 184

N

NAFTA, 100
NASA, 51
negative, influence, 92-93, 98, 99
negatives (minimizing), 102-103, 206

O

opportunity, seeking, creating, 61, 62-67, 136, 187, 238, 260
orchestra (analogy), 183-185, 190
organizational pulse, 162-163, 265, 267
ostrich syndrome, 176
others-centered, 106-107, 129, 148, 191, 192, 236, 238, 254
others-oriented, 206
Ovid, 75

P

parakletos, 127
peak performance, requiring, 167-173, 266, 269
performance indicators, 45, 160, 266
perspectives, differing, 60, 73, 74, 75-76, 124, 125, 132, 148, 217, 220, 249, 259, 262
persuasion psychology, 87
piano tuner, 154, 158, 190
pilot, 88-89, 188
Pliny the Elder, 176
positive (attitude, energy), 97-102, 103, 104, 116, 233, 235, 239, 240, 244, 245, 246
positive influence, 22, 92, 93, 94, 191, 233
possibility-minded, 223
presence, 22-23
processes, 34, 35, 52, 53, 204, 205, 217, 221
professional development *(see development)*
projection, of ideas, 79

Thank you for reading this book, and exploring the qualities of Legacy Leadership—the competencies, skills, behaviors and attitudes of great leaders of legacy. We hope you will also take the time, and make the commitment, to fully explore the Appendices which contain helpful information for becoming a Legacy Leader. There is also more information about Legacy Leadership found at the CoachWorks website at www.coachworks.com.

We sincerely invite you to let us know of any questions, concerns, or comments about this book, and about this model. We'd like to hear your stories, including the good, the bad and even the ugly of leadership experiences. If we can assist you in becoming *Legacy* Leaders, whether seasoned or emerging leaders, or entire organizations, please contact us. We will be happy to discuss the potential of partnering with you to achieve your leadership greatness—your leadership *legacy*.

Please visit our website at www.coachworks.com for more information about CoachWorks International, our products and services, and Legacy Leadership. In addition to full executive coaching services, we also offer both self and 360 feedback online assessments for Legacy Leadership.

We would enjoy hearing from all readers with any comments or questions.

CoachWorks International, Inc.
Dallas, Texas and Seattle, Washington
www.coachworks.com
www.legacyleadership.com
214.585.8254
info@coachworks.com

CPSIA information can be obtained at www.ICGtesting.com
227427LV00003B/53/P

9 780980 196504